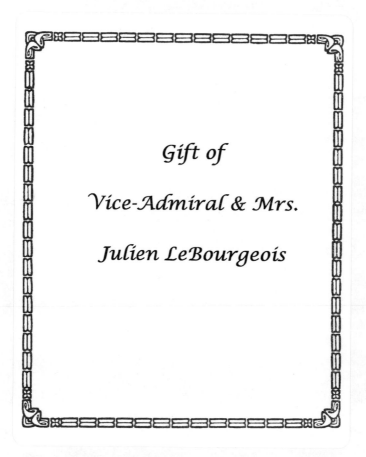

CONFEDERATE PURCHASING
OPERATIONS ABROAD

CONFEDERATE PURCHASING OPERATIONS ABROAD

BY

SAMUEL BERNARD THOMPSON

GLOUCESTER, MASS.

PETER SMITH

1973

Reprinted 1973 by Permission of
The University of North Carolina Press
ISBN: 0-8446-4055-7

To

MATTYE AND SAM

PREFACE

ALTHOUGH excellent volumes have been written on the diplomacy of the Confederacy and on blockade running during the war between the States, they do not tell the entire story of the Confederacy's trade relations. The present study represents an attempt not only to throw additional light on the Confederacy's efforts to obtain supplies from European countries and Mexico, but also to clarify and possibly correct vague impressions relative to these efforts.

Emphasis is placed on the development of the original and imperfect plan of operation abroad into a new plan which compares favorably with any achievement of the Confederate Government. This new plan involved centralization and rigid governmental control of the purchasing agents, of the shipment of cotton, of finance and blockade running. This policy was developed during the last year of the war in spite of the protests of a constituency steeped in the doctrine of State Rights. The New Plan was commented on with favor in European financial circles and the way cleared for the South to negotiate for a large foreign loan. Records of the secret negotiations for this loan reveal additional information on the so called "Kenner Mission." Although it is generally known that in 1865, Duncan F. Kenner, of Louisiana, was given unlimited authority to approach England and France on the question of emancipation in return for recognition, the fact has been overlooked that he had another mission of great importance. He was authorized by Congress to complete the negotiations for the anticipated loan. The available records do not indicate whether or not the two missions were definitely related.

This study raises the unanswerable question—would the war have ended in Southern defeat if the New Plan had been adopted one year earlier?

The author wishes to acknowledge his indebtedness to

the several members of the history department at Vanderbilt University, especially to Professor Frank L. Owsley for inspiring and directing the study; to Professor W. C. Binkley for invaluable suggestions relative to the organization of the material; to Professor Irby Hudson for aid on technical points; and, to Professor Carl S. Driver and Dr. Leota S. Driver for their friendly encouragement and careful criticism of the manuscript. He is indebted to his wife, Mattye Smalling Thompson, who was of continuous service from the time the first notes were gathered until the final proofs were read.

He wishes to thank the staffs of Vanderbilt University, the Library of Congress, and the Tennessee State Library for their generous aid.

The author wishes to express gratitude to Dr. Matthew Page Andrews, Baltimore, Maryland, for his criticism of the material and interest in its publication and to the United Daughters of the Confederacy for making the early publication of this study possible by awarding it the Mrs. Simon Baruch University Prize.

S. B. T.

Nashville, Tennessee
December, 1934

CONTENTS

CONFEDERATE PURCHASING
OPERATIONS ABROAD

CHAPTER I

THE ORIGINAL PLAN AND PERSONNEL

ONE of the ironies of history is that a nation seldom profits by the experience of another nation. In facing similar problems each becomes the victim of identical illusions and fallacious theories. Every country, as theoretical master of its own destiny, blunders along with little intelligent foresight or prophetic vision.

The Confederacy mobilized for war with the utmost confidence that the conflict would last but a few brief months. Leaders of the Southern cause failed to see the handwriting on the wall. That they faced four years of bloody strife would have seemed less reasonable to them than the sudden termination of the universe. But one should not impeach their judgment without caution. This fallacy, though it hampered her efforts at home and abroad from the beginning of the war, was not an unnatural one. It was shared by well informed statesmen in the old and the new worlds.

The South had convinced herself, as she had convinced many others, that the great nations of Europe were dependent upon her economic resources. It was believed by many that the industrial stability of France, England, and other nations was dependent on southern cotton. David Christy set forth this important philosophy in his well known book, *Cotton is King*. The idea was nurtured in the bosoms of southern gentlemen and of their children until it became an integral part of their world outlook. They reasoned that neither France nor England would allow the cotton supply to be endangered; that the wheels of world industry would cease to turn without southern cotton; that the North could not wage war successfully against a people who controlled the production of this great staple.

The King Cotton argument was used by southern states-men when negotiating for recognition and when seeking the breakdown of the blockade. The futility of their argument has been carefully analyzed,[1] and it is mentioned here only because of the bearing which it has on this treatise.

King Cotton philosophy is important for our subject from at least two points of view. First, it was a determining influence in moulding the opinion that the war would be brief, and this accepted view prevented a well devised program for securing supplies from abroad. Second, the attempt to force England and France to break the blockade by withholding cotton eliminated the only real basis for Confederate credit, namely, the shipment of cotton. The organized effort to establish credit in France and England based on cotton did not mature until the King Cotton argument was found to be a useless weapon in diplomacy.

Such munitions and supplies as were secured outside the South, during the first two or three years of the war were obtained under a haphazard plan almost incapable of identification. The scheme was improved upon from time to time until finally in 1864 a new system was perfected. The most surprising feature is that the South accomplished a great deal under the original plan, more than has been generally accepted.

Entire blame for the ill-devised method of securing foreign supplies should not be placed on the cotton philosophy. There were other and important determinants. Among them was the constant shifting of the personnel in the president's cabinet. During the entire war four men served as Secretary of State, six as Secretary of War, five as Attorney General, and two as Secretary of the Treasury. Most of the changes were made during the first two years, and during this period there was a lack of clearness in most of the Confederate policies. Policies were taking shape during these formative years and all departments suffered; it was the

[1] F. L. Owsley, *King Cotton Diplomacy*.

price paid for the creation of a new government. It took several years to evolve a government with officials who had clearly defined responsibilities. Until this could be brought about, there was considerable confusion resulting from overlapping duties and absence of definite agreements.

The selection of the first Secretary of the Treasury, the Honorable Charles G. Memminger, of South Carolina, was unfortunate. Upon his shoulders fell the heavy responsibility of financing a nation at home and overseas, without bullion or credit. He faced from the outset almost unsurmountable difficulties with a courage which did him honor. But he was neither an able financier nor a leader of men. There were no outstanding achievements of his administration. Congress lost confidence in him and eventually turned deaf ears to his recommendations. It became impossible for him to promote a financial program, and he resigned. Few historians, except his biographer, have pleaded his case.[2] He made mistakes enough, but it should be remembered that "the financial legislation of Congress was, in the most vital points, opposed to his judgment, and contrary to his often-repeated and strongly urged recommendations."[3]

Shifts in the important cabinet position of Secretary of War had an important bearing on the whole confused situation. Constant change of superior officers did not create confidence in the men struggling with the details of administration. Agents detailed by Walker, Benjamin, Randolph, or even by Myers or Gorgas, were not usually anxious to accept a change of orders from the inexperienced Seddon.[4] Conflicting orders were not only confusing but demoralizing.

By a strange turn of fate, the very principle for which the South was fighting—that of State Rights—proved to be a serious obstacle to harmonious organization and successful financial adjustment.[5] The states guarded jealously the sup-

[2] H. D. Capers, *Life and Times of C. G. Memminger.*
[3] J. C. Schwab, *The Confederate States,* p. 347.
[4] Caleb Huse, *The Supplies for the Confederate Army.*
[5] F. L. Owsley, *State Rights in the Confederacy.*

plies within their own boundaries to the disadvantage of the Confederacy. Equally as serious was their competitive policy with each other and with the Confederacy in Europe. A number of states sent their own agents abroad to purchase munitions of war. The individual states perfected no scheme for securing supplies superior to the one adopted by the Confederacy. Actually, it was consistent with the temporary plan of the Confederacy to countenance and even to encourage the efforts of the individual states to supplement their own labors.

If the plan of the Confederacy to secure supplies from abroad was not well organized during the first years of the war, the major blame may thus be placed on the following: (1) The belief that the conflict would be brief; (2) The confidence in the Confederacy that European nations would break the blockade; (3) Constant shifting of cabinet and other officers; (4) The unfortunate choice of one or more cabinet members; (5) The confusion which accompanies the formulation of any new government; (6) State Rights.

Enough has been said to emphasize the fact that the first efforts to secure supplies for the Confederacy were haphazard, and even ill advised; but, it must not be thought that there was not a plan. The temporary plan, a hand-to-mouth affair, imperfect as it was, cannot be labeled as a failure. It was not until the late months of 1864 that the New Plan was sufficiently understood and managed to indicate a radical reorganization. The fact that the Confederacy accomplished unbelievable results during the first two or three years of the war, tempts one to guess at the possible returns of a more perfect scheme during the same years. If the plan which was finally put into operation in 1864, after it was too late, had been used during the preceding years, the story of the war might be entirely different.

A brief sketch of the original plan is necessary for the study of its operation. Even the temporary plan was a gradual development. In the spring of 1861, the Ordnance

Bureau sent a young West Point graduate, a captain of artillery, to Europe with limited orders and money to purchase arms and other supplies.[6] This young man, Caleb Huse, had not yet won his spurs, but was destined to do so shortly. About six weeks after Huse left the states, the War Department dispatched an older officer, Major Edward C. Anderson, to England for two purposes: to investigate the work being done by Captain Huse, and supplant him if necessary, or to coöperate with him in the work.[7] Major Anderson was convinced of the ability of Huse, and returned to the Confederacy after a few months abroad, leaving Huse in complete control.

Before the end of the year, 1861, broader orders and duties were assigned Huse, and he began making purchases for the War Department, Ordnance Bureau, Quartermaster's Department, Medical Bureau, and in a limited way for the Navy Department. The needs of the various departments became so great during the following months that they either dispatched agents to Europe or asked permission to do so.

Meanwhile, the Navy Department, under the able leadership of Stephen D. Mallory, became active in its efforts to obtain supplies and to build ships abroad. Several officers were dispatched to Europe, among whom was the capable James D. Bulloch.[8]

In 1862 several of the individual states entered the purchasing business abroad and sent their own agents, who either carried out their instructions alone, or with the advice and coöperation of the Confederate Agents.[9]

[6] Huse, *op. cit.*, pp. 5 ff. Huse was born in Massachusetts and graduated at West Point. In 1860 he was appointed professor of chemistry and commandant of cadets at the University of Alabama. He gained recognition for his tact and courage at the University and sided with the South when the war began.

[7] *Official Records of the Union and Confederate Armies* (hereafter cited as O. R.), ser. IV, vol. I, pp. 332-33, Walker to Anderson, May 18, 1861.

[8] *Official Records of the Union and Confederate Navies* (hereafter cited as O. R. N.), ser. II, vol. II, pp. 64-65, Mallory to Bulloch, May 9, 1861. See pp. 70-72, 176-77, 254-56.

[9] O. R., ser. IV, vol. III, State Agents; O. R. N., ser. II, vol. II; Owsley, *King Cotton Diplomacy*, chaps. i-xi.

By 1862 it became more apparent that the war would be a real conflict, and efforts to secure supplies were redoubled. Officers and agents already in the field received urgent requests to speed their energies. More agents were appointed to assist in the important task. Even railroads found it expedient to have an agent represent them in foreign markets. The need for supplies became so urgent that the various departments of the Confederate Government and of the individual states made contracts with private parties and business houses in order to expedite shipments. These private contracts usually stipulated huge profits for the contractors at the expense of the government.[10]

It was discovered almost at the beginning, that the most successful method of getting supplies through the blockade was to ship them to the Sea Islands in large steamers under a neutral flag, where they were reloaded into small fast steamers for running the blockade. The goods for the War and Navy Departments were shipped almost exclusively to Nassau, Havana, and Bermuda.[11] Trusted men were appointed to these strategic points as commercial or purchasing agents to supervise the handling of supplies from other nations, and to make purchases in the islands. During the first two or three years most of the goods were shipped on privately owned vessels. The Ordnance Bureau was the one outstanding exception to this rule.[12]

Commercial Agents were appointed to the most important nations to influence public opinion, to aid in obtaining credit, and to advise with other officers and agents in the Confederate service. Their job was to create favorable sentiment, to clear the ground of impediments to trade, and to

[10] O. R., ser. IV, vols. II-IV; O. R. N., ser. II, vols. II-III, Private Contracts.

[11] James D. Bulloch, The Secret Service of the Confederate States in Europe, II, 233. C. J. Helm was sent to Cuba, Louis Heyliger to Nassau, and N. S. Walker to Bermuda. They had the control and management of the public business at these stations; the supervision of blockade-runners, distribution of pilots, arrangement for fuel, problems of finance, diplomacy and official correspondence, and actual purchases in the islands.

[12] Huse, op. cit., pp. 24 ff.

supplement the actual purchases attempted by experienced purchasing agents. In some instances they performed both duties.[13]

It was necessary to have a financial clearing house in England for the agents abroad, and the firm Fraser, Trenholm and Company, of Liverpool, was selected. This firm was associated with John Fraser and Company of Charleston, and Trenholm Brothers of New York City. The firms had an interlocking directorate, and had been associated for many years before the war. George A. Trenholm, later Secretary of the Treasury, became a senior partner in both firms by an agreement in 1853.[14]

Purchasing agents abroad usually reported to the Liverpool House for such credits as were available for their use. This firm was not one of the large banking companies in England, but it commanded respect and its interests were closely aligned with the Confederate cause. It was a happy selection, for its service to the Confederacy can hardly be overestimated. It gave all, and lost all. It was driven into bankruptcy by the North at the close of the war.[15]

Only the briefest mention of the general financial plan will be made here as it will be described in detail in another chapter. The agents, under the original plan, were sent letters of credit on the Liverpool House. Coin and exchange which the Confederacy could command were deposited with this firm. It was with this company that the funds derived from foreign loans were deposited. It became the clearing house for large shipments of cotton when the New Plan was perfected in 1864. During the second and third years of the war an occasional shipment of cotton was placed to the credit of departmental agents with Fraser, Trenholm and Company.[16] Agents in several instances secured supplies with money borrowed privately and by obtaining the

[13] Bulloch, *op. cit.*, II, 232 ff.
[14] George A. Trenholm Papers, portfolio I, 1853.
[15] Edward Willis, *Confederate Pamphlets*, No. 254; Huse, *op. cit.*, p. 25.
[16] *Ibid.;* also *O. R.*, ser. IV, vol. IV, Cotton Shipments, etc.

confidence of commercial houses. These debts, however, were liquidated through the central commercial firm.[17]

During the years 1862 and 1863 the Confederate diplomatic commissioners in Europe played an important rôle in determining the general policies of purchasing agents. In the absence of clear instructions from home, agents often looked to the Commissioners for advice. It is to be remembered that the effort abroad to secure recognition of the Confederate States colored and even determined many policies of the agents. This was especially true of decisions made by agents of the Navy Department. It was comparatively easy to buy or to build ships in England and France, but the problem of getting them on the high seas was a more delicate matter. The strategy of the Navy Department was necessarily determined by the state of diplomatic relations in the nation involved. The commissioners and the naval agents kept each other well posted. Joint effort was their only chance of success.[18]

Other agents were scarcely less dependent on the commissioners in their formulation of policy. Combined meetings of agents and commissioners were established as a part of their routine. Business concerns were more easily dealt with when the sovereignty of the Confederate States abroad, as represented by the commissioners, supported the negotiations of the individual agents. Credits could be obtained from some sources only with the endorsement of a commissioner. John Slidell in France, and James M. Mason in England, functioned most intimately with both the purchasing and the financial agents.

Sympathetic local talent was enlisted by the Confederate commissioners. Their services were especially solicited in the campaign to create favorable opinion toward the South. Occasionally European leaders were appointed commercial or financial agents. Such appointment was likely to be more

---

[17] Trenholm Papers, 1860-1865; Huse, *op. cit.*, p. 22.

[18] Bulloch, *op. cit.,*; John Bigelow, *France and the Confederate Navy;* Official correspondence in the *O. R.* and *O. R. N.*

diplomatic than practical. The most conspicuous example of this type of service was rendered by James Spence of England.[19] Spence was an author of note, as well as a prosperous business man. Considerable space will be allotted this colorful Englishman in other chapters. Confederate officials were dependent, in a large measure, on the advice of her commissioners in England and France when negotiating foreign loans. The purchasing agents could not function without money or credit. It was expected that the commissioners should be best informed on the status of public opinion abroad which would determine the probable success of a foreign loan. Upon the shoulders of Slidell and Mason fell the chief responsibility for floating and manipulating the Erlanger Loan.[20] This was the only foreign loan actually consummated during the war by the Confederacy. Some use of cotton certificates was made in England by various agents, and these certificates were negotiable only with Mason's consent and signature. In the absence, therefore, of a general financial agent in Europe during the first years of the war, the commissioners served as financial advisors for the purchasing agents, and for the government at Richmond.[21]

Thus, the original plan for securing foreign supplies, imperfect as it was, is capable of identification; and, it was gradually merged into a more perfect plan during the last eighteen months of the war.

In the whole scheme, there were numerous officers, agents, business firms, and other individuals seeking, in a more or less independent fashion, to issue orders, to determine policies, to supervise finance, to purchase supplies, and to ship them to points of safety in the Confederacy.

There were officers of the several war and navy departments appointing agents and giving orders, financing them by various methods, states and private corporations seeking

[19] Mason Papers, vols. I-VIII.
[20] Ibid., vols. II-VII; O. R. N., ser. II, vol. III, pp. 568-72; Pickett Papers, Slidell to Benjamin, October 28, 1862.
[21] Ibid.

to replenish their devastated stocks, private contractors driving hard bargains with a show of patriotism, commercial agents endeavoring to win the applause of their superiors by spectacular manipulations, commissioners acting as jacks-of-all trades, and shrewd commercial houses reaping a bountiful harvest from the supposed dangers of a paper blockade. Jealousy, conflicting orders, irrevocable mistakes were the order of the hour.   Yet, this system probably provided more supplies with less money than any other system of modern times.

CHAPTER II

PURCHASE AND SHIPMENT OF MUNITIONS

THE FIRST purchasing agent of the War Department, Caleb Huse, arrived in Liverpool on May 10, 1861, and after reporting to the financial agents of the Confederacy, Fraser, Trenholm and Company, began a thorough investigation of the possibilities of obtaining small arms, artillery, and other necessities. There were few first class arms available in Europe when the war between the states began. Such as existed were generally under the watchful eye of the several nations. It was imperative that the purchasing agents locate suitable supplies or secure contracts for their manufacture.

In conjunction with Mr. Yancey of the Confederate Commission it was decided in a very short time that the market in England afforded few arms of the character and quality which his department sought. Inquiry was made in Belgium with the same result. General Fair, former United States minister to Belgium, furnished Huse with information on this point. Fair was certain from personal inquiry that the establishments at Liege had more orders than they could fill for several months. It was also generally known throughout Europe that the Liege manufacturers were in the habit "of furnishing arms of the worst possible quality."[1]

Huse and Anderson were advised by the Confederate authorities to investigate the possibilities of securing arms in Spain.[2] Colonel Preston, former United States minister at Madrid, was in London when this suggestion was made. He was considered a friend of the Confederacy and was interviewed by the Confederate agents. Preston assured them

[1] *O. R.*, ser. IV, vol. I, p. 539, Anderson and Huse to Walker, August 11, 1861.
[2] *Ibid.*

"that it would be only throwing away time to go to Spain for weapons; that he was well acquainted with the armament of the country, and that Spain had no arms to spare, and if she had they would be found worthless."[3] They dismissed from their minds the hope of procuring supplies in Spain, but did not relax in their efforts to obtain further information regarding other possible sources.

In the meantime, negotiations were being made with the London Armory Company for the manufacture of the Enfield rifles. This company was, at that time, one of the most modern in existence, and had been under contract for supplies to the British Government for many years.[4] "Rifles made at this establishment interchange in every part and with perfect accuracy. . . . The London Armory Company is the only establishment in Europe, excepting the Government armories, that works upon this principle."[5] The monthly output of this company was about 1300 rifles, but it was still under contract to the British Government for most of these. Huse discovered that United States agents had contracted with it for "100 rifles per week for three months" and had sought an even larger contract.[6] However, the president of the company promised to break the contract with the North and to sell the entire output to the Confederacy if he could obtain a release from the British Government.[7] The Armory failed to obtain the release, and negotiations with the Company were abandoned temporarily. During the latter stages of the war the South was able to secure abundant supplies from this company.[8]

One other possible source of first class arms remained, and that was from the small factories scattered over England. During the negotiations with the London Armory,

[3] *Ibid.*
[4] *Ibid.*, p. 344, Huse to Ordnance Department, May 21, 1861.
[5] *Ibid.*   [6] Huse, *op. cit.*, p. 19.
[7] *O. R.*, ser. IV, vol. I, p. 344, Huse to Ordnance Department, May 21, 1861.
[8] Huse, *op. cit.; O. R. N.*, ser. II, vol. II, pp. 178 ff., Huse to Gorgas, April 1, 1862, etc.

Huse had cultivated the friendship of a Mr. Hamilton, senior member of the firm. Hamilton was also a member of another important English concern, Sinclair, Hamilton & Company. He was a reputable merchant and was well acquainted with the small manufacturers of England. He was also in a favorable position to compete with the agents of the Northern States in obtaining the scattered supplies. A contract was signed with Hamilton, authorizing him "to obtain as many rifles as possible . . . in consideration of receiving a commission of 2½ per cent. on the amount of the purchases."[9] This arrangement proved to be very satisfactory, and shipments of supplies to the South began in September, 1861.[10]

Having completed this arrangement in England, Huse and Anderson visited Paris to investigate the possibility of securing arms in France. Here it was reported to them by "parties said to have the control of quantities of arms . . . that they could furnish them [arms] to any limit, and that they would be of the same quality as those furnished to the French army—in fact that they would be taken direct from the French arsenals."[11] The services of Judge Rost, commissioner of the Confederate States, were enlisted. With his aid, it was soon disclosed that first class arms could not be secured in France. There was an available supply of old flint-lock muskets in France, but it was the opinion of Huse that the army would have little confidence in them.[12]

Communications and rumors were received by the agents from time to time of available supplies of cannon, small arms, and other munitions of war "of the best quality." But upon examination of the samples, they were found to be "old and unserviceable."[13] The policy of the southern agents

[9] *O. R.*, ser. IV, vol. I, pp. 539-40, Anderson and Huse to Walker, August 11, 1861.

[10] *O. R. N.*, ser. II, vol. III, p. 299, Yancey, Rost, and Mann to Russell, November 29, 1861.

[11] *O. R.*, ser. IV, vol. I, p. 540, Anderson and Huse to Walker, August 11, 1861.

[12] *Ibid.*, p. 566, Huse to Gorgas, July 22, 1861.

[13] *Ibid.*

from the beginning was to purchase first class arms only. The Enfield rifles were selected with great care, and they were of the very best. They "abstained altogether from the purchase of the old worn-out muskets that have been so greedily bought by the Northern agents." Southern agents contemplated the purchase of a number of the old muskets to prevent their falling into the hands of the North, but Huse decided these would "prove more dangerous to those who may venture to use them than to the troops against whom they are pointed."[14]   It is significant that a steady stream of the best rifles in Europe was made available for the southern army.   Shipments began as early as the fall of 1861.   Not every southern soldier was fortunate enough to obtain one of these but it is probable that enough first class arms were shipped to the South during the war to supply an army of half a million men.   It is also probable that more inferior arms fell into the hands of the northern army than the southern.   Northern agents had more money at their command, but they bought arms of every description wherever they could find them.[15]   Caleb Huse, in July, 1861, reported that the orders of the northern agents "appear to have been unlimited, both as regards price and quantity," and they paid cash in every instance.[16]

The United States agents and the agents of the individual northern states were formidable competitors.   Huse wrote Major Gorgas, on July 22, 1861, that, "the ministers to England, France, and Belgium have been very active in their endeavors to discover what the agents of the Confederacy are effecting.   They have agents employed for no other purpose, and it is of the highest importance that these agents should be kept in ignorance of all the acts of any agent of the Confederacy.   Any person that has ever become acquainted with Europe from personal experience knows how difficult it is for a stranger to keep his actions secret

[14] *Ibid.*, pp. 541, 566-67.
[15] *Ibid.*, pp. 540 ff., Anderson and Huse to Walker, August 11, 1861.
[16] *Ibid.*, p. 566, Huse to Gorgas, July 22, 1861.

when spies are on his path."[17]   A few weeks later in the joint report of Huse and Anderson to Secretary of War Walker, they state that their movements have been "very greatly embarrassed. The agents of the enemy had the advantage of precedence in time and in having at their command large sums of money for immediate operations. We had the mortification of learning every day of new contracts entered into by them for arms and accouterments, of which contracts they are now receiving the fruits. We were powerless to stop them, although we not only knew the names of the contractors, but saw the cases of goods in some instances packed and ready for shipment with the outside marks upon them."[18]   Moreover, agents of Italy, Spain, Russia, and Peru, "with large means at their command" were active in European markets.[19]

The greatest difficulty was the securing of first class rifles and cannon. Other supplies could be bought in the markets of Europe. Benjamin in his report to President Davis, in February of 1862, reported that the agents "were reduced to the necessity of contracting with manufacturers for their delivery as fast as they could be made."[20]   In the same report he states that "early attempts were also made by the Department to purchase military supplies in Canada, Cuba and Mexico . . . but these markets furnished resources too limited to be of much value."[21]   Important supplies were eventually obtained in Mexico, and a few arms of a very high grade from Cuba.

Practically all the war supplies from Europe, however, were obtained in England and France. There is one notable exception to this rule. In the spring of 1862, Caleb Huse succeeded in closing a contract with Austria for 100,000 rifles of advanced pattern, sixty pieces of field artillery "with harness complete, . . . and a quantity of ammunitions."[22]   In

[17] *Ibid.*   [18] *Ibid.*, p. 538.
[19] *Ibid.*, p. 566, Huse to Gorgas, July 22, 1861.
[20] *Ibid.*, p. 958, Benjamin to Davis, February, 1862.
[21] *Ibid.*   [22] Huse, *op. cit.*, p. 26.

spite of the protests of the United States minister and the watchful eyes of other agents, the arms were delivered and in due time shipped from Hamburg to Nassau.[23] The explanation of Austria's willingness to dispose of the artillery seems to lie in the fact that the authorities of Austria had decided on the use of gun-cotton in place of powder. She had to secure guns especially designed for gun-cotton. The field pieces which Huse purchased "were of the latest design for gunpowder."[24]

The purchase of the Austrian guns gave Huse a great deal of satisfaction, especially when he recalled the remark of Caleb Cushing that the arsenals of Europe would be closed to the South. The Austrian arsenal was considered one of the largest in Europe.[25]

During the first twelve months after the arrival of Huse in Europe, he superintended the purchase, payment and shipment of the supplies. Secretary of War Walker found it expedient to give Huse additional power as early as July 22, 1861, when he advised him in a letter, "This Department deems it necessary to enlarge your powers. . . . You are hereby instructed . . . to purchase at the earliest possible moment all the arms suitable for our purposes, . . . from whatever places and at whatever price, . . . to enter into contracts at your discretion with manufacturers and . . . sums of money, to whatever amount may be necessary, will be placed at your disposal."[26] A few weeks later, Walker again insisted that he "operate with a free and sure hand to meet our pressing needs."[27] He took Walker at his word and extended his purchases to medical supplies, quartermaster stores, and a few naval supplies. In less than a year he forwarded materials of inestimable value to the Confederacy on board the "Bermuda," "Fingal," "Stephen Hart,"

[23] Ibid.; O. R. N., ser. II, vol. II, pp. 177 ff., Huse to Gorgas, April 1, 1862; O. R., ser. IV, vol. I, p. 1005.

[24] Huse, op. cit., p. 27.

[25] Ibid.

[26] O. R., ser. IV, vol. I, pp. 493-94.

[27] Ibid., p. 594 (August 30, 1861).

"Gladiator," "Economist," "Southwick," "Minna," "Bahama," and the "Melita." Only the "Stephen Hart," a sailing vessel, was captured. He had spent not less than two and a quarter millions of dollars and owed half a million more.[28]

The cargoes of the above ships consisted mostly of Enfield rifles, revolvers, bayonets, swords, cannon, powder, cartridges, leather, medical stores, cloth, shoes, blankets, and sundry accouterments.[29] A volume could be written concerning the voyage and final destiny of these first ships from Europe to the Confederacy with munitions of war; but only a few points have direct bearing on our story.

The British steamer, "Bermuda," was the first to leave England, and she arrived in Savannah on September 28, 1861.[30] Most of the munitions belonged to private owners[31] and were shipped under the direction of Fraser, Trenholm and Company.[32] There was a mad scramble by state representatives of Georgia and of South Carolina[33] to obtain possession of them. The materials for clothing on board the "Bermuda" were bought by the Quartermaster's department from the private owners. The department believed it paid exorbitant rates for this material and immediately started agitation to send a purchasing agent to Europe for the Quartermaster's department.[34] It was not until July of the next year that its request was granted.

In October, 1861, the screw-steamship, "Fingal," which had been purchased by Captain Bulloch, left England under his command. This was the first ship to run the blockade solely on Government account, and no single ship ever car-

[28] *Ibid.*, pp. 564-65, 594 ff., 985, 1115 ff.

[29] *Ibid.*, pp. 615-88, 800-811, 895-98, 1003-5, 1017-57; Bulloch, *op. cit.*, I, 110-12; O. R., ser. II, vol. III, p. 461; Francis B. C. Bradlee, *Blockade Running during the Civil War*, pp. 21 ff.; O. R. N., ser. II, vol. II, pp. 177 ff.; and III, 290-99.

[30] *Ibid.*, p. 299, Yancey, Rost, and Mann to Russell, November 29, 1861.

[31] O. R., ser. IV, vol. I, p. 615, Benjamin to Brown, September 20, 1861.

[32] *Ibid.*, p. 614, J. R. Gist to Benjamin, September 18, 1861; Bulloch, *op. cit.*, I, 70 ff.

[33] O. R., ser. IV, vol. I, pp. 614, 667, 668 ff.

[34] *Ibid.*, p. 688, Myers to Benjamin, October 10, 1861.

ried into the Confederacy a cargo so entirely composed of military and naval supplies.[35] To make this shipment available for the Confederate army covering Richmond was especially desirable. It was necessary, therefore, to get it into a harbor which had railway connections with Virginia. Savannah was decided upon. A set of signals were prepared and sent to Savannah in advance. These signals "were secreted by removing the wrapper of a well-made cigar and carefully replacing it, after rolling the paper containing the signals upon its body,"[36] a bit of work performed by Caleb Huse. The "Fingal" was safely anchored at Savannah, November 12, 1861.[37] On this ship Major Anderson returned to the Confederacy after becoming satisfied that Huse was capable of supervising the purchase of munitions.

By the time the "Fingal" had reached Savannah, another ship, the "Gladiator" had been loaded by Caleb Huse in England with a million dollars' worth of supplies.[38] Arrangements for this vessel were made with Fraser, Trenholm and Company.[39] This boat was a slow screw-steamer but was much better than the sailing vessel which was first considered for the shipment.[40] The "Gladiator" left England on November 10, and arrived at Nassau on December 9.[41] There the cargo was reshipped in small fast steamers through the blockade and the Confederate Government received it in full by March, 1862.[42]

The method adopted in regard to the cargo of the "Gladiator" was repeated in the handling of many other shipments, that is, "cargoes were sent out to Nassau, and were there transshipped, sometimes directly, from vessel to vessel, in the harbor, sometimes after being landed on the

[35] Bulloch, op. cit., I, 111-12.

[36] Huse, op. cit., p. 32.

[37] Bulloch, op. cit., I, 127.

[38] Ibid., O. R., ser. IV, vol. I, p. 817.

[39] Ibid., for contract and agreement between Huse and Stock, October 24, 1861.

[40] Ibid., p. 806, Helm to Benjamin, December 21, 1861.

[41] Ibid., p. 810-11, Hoyt to John Fraser and Co., December 20, 1861.

[42] Ibid., p. 985, Benjamin to Huse, March 10, 1862.

wharf; and thence were transported in a new conveyance to the blockaded port. Return cargoes were transshipped in the same way."[43] This method had several advantages. It made the continuity of the transaction much more difficult of proof. It enabled the traders to use heavy freighters for the voyage across the Atlantic, and light swift steamers for blockade running.

The only one of the first shipments to be captured was on board the "Stephen Hart." She was "a schooner of American build, but purchased by an English house and put under the British flag for Confederate use."[44] The vessel was loaded with army supplies destined for the Confederacy, and left Liverpool in November, 1861.[45] "Stephen Hart" was captured and confiscated by the United States, for the proof was complete that she was loaded with army supplies destined for the Confederate States.[46] This episode convinced Huse that it was a mistake to ship such supplies by sailing vessels, and the error was not repeated.[47]

Caleb Huse was forced to act almost single handed in the purchase and shipment of supplies during 1861 and the early months of 1862. During 1862 the Confederate organization abroad became more complex. The form which it took during this year was maintained until the reorganization which was perfected in 1864. Huse continued as the chief agent for the War Department and was promoted to the rank of major in recognition of his services. But, other important men became active in 1862.

Henry Hotze arrived in London on January 29, 1862,[48] with orders to cultivate friendly sentiment toward the Confederacy, to coöperate with the purchasing agents, and to impress upon the agents the urgent need of supplies.[49]

[43] J. R. Soley, *The Blockade and the Cruisers*, p. 39.
[44] Huse, *op. cit.*, p. 24.
[45] *O. R.*, ser. IV, vol. I, p. 898, Moore to Benjamin, January 31, 1862.
[46] *Ibid.*, p. 985, Benjamin to Huse, March 10, 1862; also Huse, *op. cit.*, p. 24.   [47] *Ibid.*
[48] Pickett Papers, Hotze to Secretary of State, No. 2, February 1, 1862.
[49] *O. R.*, ser. IV, vol. I, p. 596, Walker to Hotze, August 31, 1861; *O. R. N.*, ser. II, vol. III, pp. 293-94, Hunter to Hotze, November 14, 1861.

Hotze served the agents in an advisory capacity, and was helpful in the negotiations for credit. The problem of financial credits was so inseparably connected with the whole foreign policy of the Confederacy and it formed such a large ingredient of public opinion that Hotze was gradually drawn into close relationship with the purchasing agents.[50] Hotze's activity was primarily as press agent and propagandist in behalf of the Confederacy, and in this type of effort he was almost without a superior. But his work was enlarged as his capacities became known, and he gained the confidence of influential men abroad. His dispatches to the Confederacy carried considerable weight, and his advice was often followed by Confederate officials.[51]

John Slidell and James Mason arrived in London on the same day that Hotze did. Slidell at once proceeded to Paris. Henceforth, these two men became the chief advisors of the purchasing agents abroad, especially on problems of finance and policy.

The staff of purchasing agents was enlarged in 1862. Major J. B. Ferguson was sent abroad by the quartermaster's department at the urgent request of the Quartermaster-General.[52] In December, the semi-private contract with William G. Crenshaw to purchase supplies was signed by the Confederacy.[53] During the winter of 1862-1863 numerous agreements were signed by the Confederacy with private contractors. State agents also made their appearance. During the years 1861-1862, the Navy Department dispatched its most effective purchasing agents. In February, 1862, James Bulloch, by a well-earned promotion, became the recognized leader of the naval agents.[54] James Spence was

[50] Pickett Papers, Hotze's Correspondence with Secretary of State, Nos. 1-49, especially No. 30. See also Schwab, op. cit.
[51] O. R. N., ser. II, vol. III, pp. 659-60, Benjamin to Hotze, January 16, 1863.
[52] O. R., ser. IV, vol. II, p. 133, Randolph to Memminger, October 20, 1862.
[53] Ibid., pp. 244 ff., Seddon to Mason, December 18, 1862; Mason Papers, December 18, 1862 and March 20, 1863.
[54] O. R. N., ser. II, vol. II, p. 236, Bulloch to Mallory, August 11, 1862.

appointed European financial agent by Benjamin in October, 1862, upon the nomination of James Mason earlier in the year.[55]

Thus it took the Confederacy a year and a half to evolve an organized program for securing supplies from Europe. The organization, even at this time and for many months yet to come, remained a comparatively loose one. Duties and responsibilities were not clearly defined, and the business of purchasing, shipping, and financing continued in a haphazard fashion, each agent working more or less independently. There was no central authority, even in the most important matter of finance. True, Spence had been named financial agent, but the designation proved to be practically meaningless, or at best honorary. Any honor attached to it was eventually taken away from him.

The Ordnance Bureau, with Colonel Gorgas at its head, and Caleb Huse as his trusted agent, probably functioned most effectively. Huse continued to make purchases for other departments, but his chief interest was in behalf of his trusted Chief of Ordnance. Huse had made an early contract with the English firm, Isaac, Campbell and Company, through which most of the supplies were bought. This London firm enabled Huse to continue shipments of supplies long after available funds were exhausted. Some four and a half or five million dollars worth of supplies had been purchased through Isaac, Campbell and Company by the end of 1862,[56] and it had received from Huse slightly more than fifty per cent of the amount due.[57] This company was discredited before the end of the war because it was keeping a double set of books for Confederate accounts, and charged a sizeable commission for the services. It expected to make a large profit but the risk was considered great. Yet, there was much truth in the statement made by its representative

[55] Mason Papers, Mason to Benjamin, No. 9.
[56] Schwab, *op. cit.*, p. 29.
[57] *O. R. N.*, ser. II, vol. III, p. 605, Hart to Benjamin, November 17, 1862; Pickett Papers, Hart to Benjamin, January 13, 1863.

in a letter to Benjamin on January 13, 1863, "Since the very incipiency of the struggle in which the Confederate States have been and continue to be engaged we have afforded them every assistance in our power and we refer with unmixed satisfaction to the testimonials and kind acknowledgments from yourself when administering the War Department of the services we have rendered to the State in the infancy of the war when our resources in money and credit were placed without limit at its disposal and probably contributed in some degree to the success of its armies in the field."[58]

The significance of the services rendered by this company is that it helped the Confederacy when no one else was willing to take the risk. Careful study of its reports and a comparison with other contracts indicate that it sought to profit less than many so-called patriotic southern contractors. The alliance with Huse brought it nothing but grief and bankruptcy.[59]

The Ordnance Bureau first tried the experiment of blockade running on government account. Huse purchased four steamers abroad, the "Columbia," "R. E. Lee," "Merrimac," and the "Eugenie." Gorgas negotiated for the "Phantom" at home. These ships were successful in running the blockade with supplies and slipping out again with cotton.[60] It is significant that from September 30, 1862, to September 30, 1863, these steamers imported in addition to leather, flannel, Blakely guns, and other supplies, four times as many small arms as were produced at the combined armories at Richmond, Fayetteville and Asheville.[61] It is to be remembered that the need for small arms was pressing throughout the war. More significant, however, was the example it set for the War and Navy Departments. It was a practical demonstration that the government did not have to depend on privately owned vessels, which charged ex-

[58] *Ibid.* Hart was a representative of Isaac, Campbell and Company at Nassau.
[59] *O. R.,* ser. IV, vol. II, pp. 885 ff. with inclosures.
[60] *Ibid.,* pp. 955 ff., Gorgas' report to Seddon, November 15, 1863.
[61] *Ibid.,* p. 956.

orbitant rates, for blockade running. It was a long time before the Government decided to profit by the lesson and to enter the business on a large scale.

While Huse was tenaciously carrying out his own program, Ferguson and Crenshaw were finding their plans somewhat blocked by the failure of Huse to coöperate with them. As a matter of fact, Huse did not approve of the Crenshaw Contract;[62] and in the absence of authority to nullify it, he resorted to all sorts of tricks to delay it. This procedure drew severe criticism from Crenshaw, Collie and Company, Ferguson, Seddon, and Mason.[63]

Crenshaw declared that Huse not only refused to aid him but worked in direct opposition.[64] Collie and Company declared that "Huse is not only unbusinesslike but discreditable and disgraceful in the highest degree,"[65] and finally that "I find it impossible to put any confidence in Major Huse and as he has been appointed to the chief command here of the Ordnance and Quartermaster's Department I must ask you to relieve me of any farther coöperation."[66]

The correspondence of Huse with Crenshaw was usually brief and very cool. Early in April, 1863, Huse wrote to Crenshaw that he would inform him of the needs of the War Department, but "As regards the purchase of supplies for the Ordnance and Medical Department, I shall make the purchases without availing myself of the services of Messrs. Crenshaw & Collie, excepting in such cases as I may feel satisfied their agency would be advantageous to the Confederate States Government."[67]

Crenshaw and Collie soon discovered that Huse did not encourage their services. Huse finally told Crenshaw that he believed the contract should be cancelled and refused to

---

[62] Details of this contract, Mason Papers, V, 917, March, 1863.

[63] Ibid., pp. 973 ff.; O. R., ser. IV, vols. I-II.

[64] Mason Papers, V, 973, 980, 981, 985, and passim; Crenshaw to Mason, April 15, 1863.

[65] Ibid., p. 1076, June 11, 1863.

[66] Ibid., Collie and Company to Crenshaw, June 11, 1863.

[67] O. R., ser. IV, vol. II, p. 482, Huse to Crenshaw, April 11, 1863.

advance Crenshaw any money. At this Crenshaw flew into a rage.[68] He appealed to J. A. Seddon, Secretary of War, and Seddon answered Crenshaw that he regretted the embarrassment caused by the existing relations but reminded him that he was among those who had suggested that one agent supervise purchases abroad. Furthermore, "the selection of Major Huse for this purpose was naturally induced by the position he already held, and the fact that the chief purchases of the Department abroad had heretofore been made by him."[69] Seddon had already stated that all the terms agreed to between Mason, Crenshaw and Collie were not to his liking.[70] The reasons which Huse had given Crenshaw for not entering cordially into the relationship had been forwarded to Seddon. These Huse had summarized as follows: first, no official instructions had been given him (Huse) to carry out the contract; second, the Government (Ordnance Department) had several steamers engaged in running the blockade, and these steamers would be idle if the purchasing and forwarding of ordnance and medical supplies were turned over to Crenshaw; third, some of the principal articles were being purchased by Huse direct from the manufacturers at a saving to the Government; fourth, Crenshaw had associated himself with a house (Collie and Company), "inexperienced in the purchasing of army supplies"; fifth, "to make any serious change in the conduct of the business of purchasing and forwarding supplies for the Confederate States Government, which has been successfully carried on since the war commenced, could not fail to be attended with inconvenience, if not loss, to the Government."[71] Seddon was slow to criticise the actions of Huse, but his implicit faith in Crenshaw eventually motivated him to ask for an investigation of Huse's activities and finally to censure him severely.

[68] *Ibid.*, p. 540, Crenshaw to Huse, April 27, 1863. See also Huse's letters to Crenshaw, April 14 and 16.
[69] *Ibid.*, pp. 599-602, Seddon to Crenshaw, June 21, 1863.
[70] *Ibid.*, pp. 565-67, Seddon to Crenshaw, May 23, 1863.
[71] *Ibid.*, pp. 537-38, Huse to Crenshaw, April 14, 1863.

Similar reports reached the Confederacy concerning Huse and his failure to coöperate with other agents. De Leon, in France, notified the Secretary of State of the strange actions of Huse in regard to the fulfillment of a contract with the French firm, C. Girard and Company.[72] J. B. Ferguson, special agent for the Quartermaster-General, complained of Huse and wrote Myers in April. "If you desire me to remain out here I ask to be allowed to control the means intended to be used for the Quartermaster's Department, every cent of which will be accounted for properly."[73] It has already been noted that James Mason had no special liking for Huse. With Seddon, Crenshaw, Ferguson, De Leon, and Mason against him, the case looked hopeless for Huse.

Myers, on the basis of Ferguson's testimony, wrote Seddon, May 16, "I deem it a duty to express my unwillingness that Major Huse should continue to be an agent of this department."[74] Ferguson had accused Huse of receiving a commission from Isaac, Campbell and Company.[75] Huse even admitted that he had received a commission but stated that he had used a part of the money for travelling expenses, and a part for a military library "which he intended to present to the Ordnance Department."[76] Huse later told Mason that he intended to spend the commission as stated above, but "finding the Government so much pressed for money, he had paid the amount over to the credit of his account with Isaac, Campbell & Company."[77]

Huse retained the confidence of John Slidell, Josiah Gorgas, and S. P. Moore, Surgeon-General of the Confederate States' army.[78] Gorgas was especially active in the defense of Huse. In a letter criticising Myers for accepting

[72] Pickett Papers, De Leon to Secretary of State, No. 6, February 23, 1863.
[73] O. R., ser. IV, vol. II, p. 557, Ferguson to Myers, April 18, 1863.
[74] Ibid., pp. 555-56, Myers to Seddon, May 16, 1863.
[75] Ibid., pp. 556-57, Ferguson to Myers, April 18, 1863.
[76] Ibid.
[77] Ibid., 544-45, Crenshaw to Seddon, May 5, 1863.
[78] Ibid., p. 564; III, 158.

Ferguson's testimony without investigation, he set forth his own position concerning Huse. He declared that the matter of a commission could be explained by Huse; that no doubt Huse had to pay over-market value for goods, but that, "Purchases at those rates have saved my department and that of the Quartermaster-General millions of dollars if compared with the charges made by Confederate houses at Confederate ports,"[79] and that he and Moore were satisfied with his (Huse's) services and desired no change.[80] However, Huse was directed, at his own request, to confine his purchases to the Ordnance and Medical Departments. Huse expressed regret at ever making purchases for the Quartermaster's Department.[81]

Ferguson and Crenshaw were persistent in their efforts to undermine Huse, apparently for two reasons: first, he had blocked contracts which they wished to make; and second, they wished to get all the business from under his jurisdiction. They pointed out that Isaac, Campbell and Company had once been an agent for the British Government but in May, 1858 was dismissed for fraud,[82] and that several Confederate officials were suspicious of the dealings of the firm with Huse.[83] Furthermore, Lieutenant James H. North of the Navy Department had been approached by the senior partner in the firm with an offer to split a commission with him.[84] Crenshaw and Ferguson drew their own conclusions based on these facts. A thorough investigation of the matter was ordered. Huse requested an audit of the Isaac, Campbell & Company accounts.[85] Crenshaw and Ferguson were requested to repeat their charges in detail.[86] General C. J. McRae, agent for the Erlanger loan, was appointed to conduct the investigation.

[79] Ibid., II, 564, Gorgas to Seddon, May 22, 1863.
[80] Ibid.   [81] Ibid.
[82] Ibid., pp. 543-44, Crenshaw to Seddon, May 5, 1863.
[83] Ibid.; also pp. 1067-68.
[84] Mason Papers, V, 923. North explains the proposition. See also O. R., ser. IV, vol. II, p. 558, North to Ferguson, April 1, 1863.
[85] Ibid., p. 644, Gorgas to Seddon, July 18, 1863.
[86] Ibid., pp. 892-93, McRae to Ferguson and Crenshaw, October 16, 1863.

Huse welcomed the chance to clear himself. In reply to a letter from McRae informing him that Ferguson and Crenshaw had been asked to substantiate their charges against him, he wrote McRae on October 20, "I have not only been personally annoyed by the conduct of Major Ferguson and Mr. Crenshaw, but my efficiency as an agent of the C. S. War Department has been seriously impaired to such an extent that my character for integrity and soundness of judgment should be fully re-established; or failing this, that some other officer should be detailed for the important duty to which I have been assigned."[87]

In the meantime, Huse had secured a provisional contract in France for 100,000,000 francs worth of supplies including six ships.[88] Crenshaw redoubled his efforts against Huse when he heard of the French contract.[89] Efforts were made to prove that Huse was being bribed in France. An article attributed to Mr. Charles Lamar which appeared in the New York *Herald* stated that Major Huse "is said 'to have received from his English friends a country house at Auteuil, near Paris, where he lives in great style.' "[90]

Against this charge, John Slidell and Erlanger and Company, defended him. Erlanger wrote McRae, "I think it my duty to inform you that the country house where Major Huse lives is mine; that I am owner of several country houses in Auteuil which I do not like to let, and that I have offered Major Huse and Colonel Bulloch the use of one of these houses. . . ."[91] Erlanger also mentioned the fact that in the early negotiations in regard to the Erlanger Loan he had offered Huse a commission to take the proposition through the blockade to the Confederate Government, but that he would not accept the offer.[92]

John Slidell advised McRae that Huse impressed him

[87] *Ibid.*, p. 893, Huse to McRae, October 20, 1863.

[88] Mason Papers, VI, 1152; I, 169; also Mason's letter to Slidell, July 8, 1863; Pickett Papers, Slidell to Benjamin, No. 47, October 25, 1862.

[89] *O. R.*, ser. IV, vol. II, pp. 628-30, Crenshaw to Mason, July 14, 1863.

[90] *O. R.*, ser. IV, Vol. III, p. 158, Erlanger to McRae, February 13, 1864.

[91] *Ibid.*   [92] *Ibid.*

most favorably, that he lived "with great simplicity and economy in the suburbs of Paris," and that he always seemed to be "animated by an anxious desire to perform most scrupulously and consistently the duties intrusted to him."[93]

Audit of the books of Isaac, Campbell and Company convinced McRae that it had in many instances made fraudulent charges.[94]   Confederate officials henceforth dealt with the Company in the severest possible terms, in spite of the tremendous service which it had rendered the Confederacy. But Huse was acquitted of any charge of "intentional error and malfeasance," and testimony was given to his zeal, energy, and personal honor.[95]   McRae and Bloodgood went so far as to suggest additional pay for Huse.[96]   Huse continued in the Confederate Government throughout the war and continued to make large purchases of ordnance stores.[97]

Long before the final settlement with Isaac, Campbell and Company, McRae decided that the Crenshaw and Collie contract was not favorable to the government, and he took steps to annul it.[98]   Collie and Company and Crenshaw had not worked together harmoniously.[99]   New contracts were made, one with A. Collie and Company, and a separate one with Crenshaw.   Crenshaw had his purchases confined to commissary stores.[100]   Before the end of the war[101] Collie and Company made a fortune out of their venture.

During several months of 1863, the activity of the agents came practically to a standstill.   One reason was the lack of harmony just described, and the other was the course of the

[93] *Ibid.*, Slidell to McRae, February 14, 1864.

[94] *Ibid.*, p. 528, McRae to Seddon, July 4, 1864.

[95] *Ibid.*, p. 704, Campbell to Seddon, December 30, 1864.

[96] *Ibid.*, p. 703, McRae and Bloodgood to Seddon, October 1, 1864.

[97] Trenholm Papers, portfolio I.   See reports of drafts for October and December, 1864.

[98] *O. R.*, ser. IV, vol. III, pp. 525-29, McRae to Seddon, July 4, 1864.

[99] Mason Papers, VI, 1220, Collie to Mason, December 10, 1863, accuses Crenshaw of having a "nasty jealous spirit."

[100] *O. R.*, ser. IV, vol. III, pp. 525-29, McRae to Seddon, July 4, 1864; Mason Papers, VI, 1220.

[101] Trenholm Papers, portfolio I; Mason Papers, vols. VI-VII.

Erlanger Loan. In the spring of 1863 at a general conference of the agents, Spence, Prioleau, Maury, Bulloch,
North, Huse, and Ferguson, it was agreed to suspend financial activity until the outcome of the loan could be determined. By the end of the year McRae had become the
commanding officer of the agents in Europe. A new plan of
operation was developed and rapidly perfected during 1864.
The evolution of this plan shall be discussed in other chapters.

Agents for the Confederate Navy Department were dispatched to Europe as rapidly as possible after the beginning
of hostilities. The needs of the department were unlimited,
for the South had few ships, no collection of material for
ship building, no machine shops, and no yards.[102] James D.
Bulloch was the first and remained the chief agent of the
navy in Europe throughout the war. He made arrangements for supplies ranging from lead pencils to iron-clads.
James II. North was sent on a special mission to secure iron-
clads. George T. Sinclair, M. F. Maury, John Wilkinson,
and John N. Moffitt also served the Navy Department as
special agents at one time or another.[103]

In the purchase and shipment of naval supplies, the navy
agents followed the same methods as pursued by the agents
of the War Department. The supplies were purchased
chiefly in England and France[104] and shipped to the Sea
Islands where they were loaded into blockade runners bound
for Confederate ports.

The first orders to the navy agents called for extensive
purchases of arms and ammunition,[105] but as soon as the
plan to build gun-boats at home was put into operation,
orders were sent for every description of naval supplies, as

[102] Bulloch, *op. cit.*, I, 46.

[103] O. R. N., ser. II, vol. II; Mason Papers; Pickett Papers.

[104] O. R. N., ser. II, vol. II, pp. 664-65, 668-69, 671-72, and *passim* for
miscellaneous equipment bought in France; *ibid.*, p. 769 for supplies bought
in England. See O. R., ser. IV, vols. II and III for sundry supplies; also
Bulloch, *op. cit.*, vol. I.

[105] *Ibid.*, II, 216; O. R. N., ser. II, vol. II, pp. 64-65, Mallory to Bulloch,
May 9, 1861.

well as for such items as iron, tools, engines, and special ordnance stores.

The chief work of Bulloch and his associates was the purchase and construction of various types of ships. The problem of building ships, especially iron-clads, at home was practically insurmountable. It was suggested early in the war that such an attempt be made, but at that time it seemed very probable no special difficulty would be experienced in obtaining them in England or France. It is true, however, that the policy of building ships at home gathered momentum as the war progressed. The success of the Merrimac spurred Confederate authorities to build iron-cased vessels at Charleston, New Orleans, Savannah, Wilmington, Richmond, and on the inland waters of southern states.[106] But the best of the iron cased vessels constructed within the Confederate States were poor specimens as compared with a first class iron-clad.[107]

The ships first ordered by Mallory, Secretary of the Navy, were high class cruisers. Instructions to Bulloch called for six steam propellers, designed for extensive cruisers.[108] The purposes of such vessels were first, to destroy the commerce of the enemy; and second, to compel the United States Navy to send some of their best ships abroad for pursuit purposes, thereby increasing their naval expenses and weakening the blockade.[109] The second class of vessels were the iron-clads. The South was early aware of the construction in the North of vessels such as the "Monitor." Mallory was convinced of the great need of boats to match them, to open and protect blockaded ports, and to harass the port cities of the enemy.[110] Iron-clads had already played an important part in the naval policy of England and France. Mallory succeeded in convincing Congress in May,

[106] Bulloch, *op. cit.*, vol. II, chap. iv.
[107] *Ibid.*, II, 205 ff.
[108] *O. R. N.*, ser. II, vol. II, pp. 64-65, Mallory to Bulloch, May 9, 1861.
[109] Bulloch, *op. cit.*, II, 197 ff.; I, 46 ff.
[110] *O. R. N.*, ser. II, vol. II, pp. 67-69, Mallory to Conrad, May 10, 1861; Bulloch, *op. cit.*, II, 201.

1861, that the needs for iron-cased vessels was urgent. Congress immediately voted two million dollars for the purchase or construction of two iron clads[111] and Lieutenant James H. North was commissioned to go to Europe to supervise the transaction.[112] The third class of ships sought by the Navy agents especially during the last year of the war was commercial vessels and blockade runners.[113]

After a few months in England, Bulloch was convinced that cruisers of the type which he sought could not be obtained. He therefore contracted for the construction of the "Oreto" or "Florida," and the "Alabama."[114] In these negotiations he moved with the utmost secrecy for the espionage system of the United States Consular agents was developed early in the war. Private detectives and spies maintained a vigilant watch over the dock-yards and the movements of Confederate agents.[115] England was scarcely less thorough in her investigation of all ships under construction, and the care which she took to prevent any infringement of the Foreign Enlistment Act was rigid to the slightest detail.

Such pressure made it necessary to dispatch the "Florida" to Nassau in the spring of 1862, to complete her equipment.[116] The "Alabama" escaped just in time to avoid the order of Lord Russell to stop her.[117]

In the meantime, Lieutenant North, after much delay and bitter disappointment, had succeeded in closing a contract with James and George Thomson of Glasgow for a giant iron-clad.[118] This ship was the most formidable ever

---

[111] *Ibid.*, pp. 66-67.

[112] *Ibid.*, pp. 70-72, Mallory to North, May 17, 1861.

[113] *Ibid.*, pp. 617 ff., Wilkinson to Mallory, March 27, 1864; Trenholm Papers, portfolio I; Bulloch, *op. cit.*, II, 237 ff.

[114] *O. R. N.*, ser. II, vol. II, pp. 83 ff.

[115] Bulloch, *op. cit.*, I, 102; Owsley, *King Cotton Diplomacy*, p. 421; *O. R. N.*, ser. II, vol. II, pp. 183-85; Bulloch to Mallory, April 11, 1862, pp. 166-68; North to Mallory, March 6, 1862.

[116] *Ibid.*; also pp. 147, 204-5.

[117] Mason Papers, vol. III, Bulloch to Mason, September 1, 1862; and IV, 721, Bulloch to Mason, August 24, 1862.

[118] *O. R. N.*, ser. II, vol. II, pp. 191-204, May 20-21, 1862.

constructed by the Confederacy. It was to cost when completed £182,000 and had a tonnage of 3,200 tons.[119]

Bulloch still insisted that "the cheapest, and by far the speediest, mode of getting out iron[clad] fleet for the protection of our harbors and rivers would be to build the hulls of wood in the Confederate ports and send over working plans from which the plates, bolts, etc., could be made here and sent over in lots, properly assorted and marked."[120] The time element was important, and North had already reported that it took two years to build "iron-clads" the size of the "Warrior."[121] Fifteen months for the construction of an iron-clad was considered fast time.[122] The Thomson brothers promised to deliver the iron-clad to North in about twelve months.[123]

The suggestion of Bulloch that iron-clads be built in the Confederacy did not attract favorable attention at first, because the Government believed that the tone of Mr. Seward's dispatches to United States ministers abroad, and the harsh policy of the United States cruisers toward neutral commerce, would so arouse European opposition that neutrality laws would not be strictly enforced.[124] Orders were forwarded to Bulloch in the spring of 1862 to negotiate for other iron-clads. A contract was promptly signed with John Laird and Sons, who were building the "Alabama," for two iron-clads to cost £93,750 each. They were to be delivered in March and May 1863.[125]

Before the iron-clads contracted for by Bulloch and North were completed, a series of events made it evident that no iron-clads would ever leave the ports of England.

The disaster inflicted upon the commerce of the Northern States by the "Alabama," precipitated an insistent demand

[119] *Ibid.*, pp. 193-99.
[120] *Ibid.*, p. 192, Bulloch to North, May 18, 1862.
[121] *Ibid.*, p. 87, North to Mallory, August 16, 1861.
[122] *Ibid.*, p. 193, Bulloch to North, May 18, 1862.
[123] *Ibid.*, p. 199 (contract signed May 21, 1862, vessel to be delivered June 1, 1863).
[124] Bulloch, *op. cit.*, I, 383.   [125] *Ibid.*, p. 386.

by the United States for damages, which in turn colored the whole policy of England toward ships being built in her ports. This change of policy may be noted in the "Alexandra" case. The gun-boat, "Alexandra," was contracted for by Fraser, Trenholm and Company, who intended it as a gift to the Confederacy.[126] She was being built by Fawcett, Preston and Company, who built the "Florida,"[127] a coincidence which made the United States Consul very uneasy about her final destination. It had been the opinion of leading barristers in England before contracts for the "Florida," and "Alabama" were made that it was not illegal for "a builder to build, or a purchaser to buy, a ship of any description whatever, provided she was not armed for war and no men were enlisted or engaged to go in her for the service of a foreign state."[128]

The American minister secured affidavits which enabled him to affirm that the "Alexandra" was destined for the Confederacy.[129] After prolonged correspondence between Mr. Adams and Lord Russell the ship was seized on April 5, 1863, and a suit entered in the Court of Exchequer for her forfeiture to the Crown.[130] This proved to be a test case for the exposition of the Foreign Enlistment Act. The "Alexandra" was seized on the basis of suspicion, rather than on positive evidence. There was not sufficient evidence at the trial to prove that the "Alexandra" was destined for the Confederacy, but the policy of seizure on suspicion placed a new impediment in the way of Confederate agents.[131] The affair of the "Alexandra" made the agents uneasy and Confederate officials were forced to be more cautious.[132]

By July 18, 1863, considerable information had been gathered by the United States agents regarding the iron-

---

[126] *O. R. N.*, ser. II, vol. II, pp. 444 ff., Bulloch to Mallory, June 30, 1863.
[127] Bulloch, *op. cit.*, vol. I, chap. iv; Mason Papers, vols. VI-VIII.
[128] Bulloch, *op. cit.*, I, 330. See Mason Papers, VIII, 1544-57 for Confederate interpretation.
[129] Bulloch, *op. cit.*, I, 330.
[130] *O. R. N.*, ser. II, vol. II, pp. 447 ff.
[131] Bulloch, *op. cit.*, I, 338 ff.   [132] Mason Papers, VI, 1174.

clads being built by Laird and Company. Adams protested to Lord Russell, but Russell claimed there was insufficient evidence for action. Finally, in September, 1863, Adams assured Russell that positive action by England in detaining the iron-clads was necessary to prevent an open breach with his government. Three days later Russell wrote Adams that "instructions have been issued which will prevent the departure of the two iron-clad vessels from Liverpool."[133]

An attempt was made by Bulloch and Slidell to secure the ships through Messrs. A. Bravay and Company of France, who were to buy them ostensibly for the Pasha of Egypt. It was expected that England might release the ships as the property of French subjects.[134] Slidell believed the Emperor would act if needs be to complete such a transaction. But the Emperor refused to intervene. In February, 1864, Bulloch, John Slidell, James Mason, and Captain Barron decided there was no hope of getting the ships out. They decided, therefore, to sell them as soon as possible.[135] The Navy Department was reluctant to give up the iron-clads, even with the danger of forfeiture, but a few months later gave Bulloch orders to dispose of them.[136]

Lieutenant North and George T. Sinclair had no better success in Scotland. North was forced to leave Glasgow, and he gave orders to sell his ship to prevent its being seized by the British Government.[137] The screw steamer "Pampero," which Sinclair had under construction, was seized in December, 1863.[138]

"Lieutenant George T. Sinclair arrived in England on special service, his orders being to build, if possible, a vessel

[133] For full account of this episode see Owsley, *King Cotton Diplomacy*, chap. xiii; Mason Papers, vols. VI-VIII; and Bulloch, *op. cit.*, vol. I.

[134] *O. R. N.*, ser. II, vol. II, pp. 508-11, Bulloch to Mallory, October 20, 1863.

[135] *Ibid.*, pp. 585-86, Bulloch to Mallory, February 17, 1864.

[136] *Ibid.*, pp. 709-10, Bulloch to Mallory, August 25, 1864.

[137] *Ibid.*, p. 587, North to Mallory, February 18, 1864; Bulloch, *op. cit.*, II, 271.

[138] *O. R. N.*, ser. II, vol. II, p. 566, North to Mallory, December 14, 1863; Bulloch, *op. cit.*, vol. II, chap. iv.

suited for a cruiser, and to go to sea in command of her himself. In pursuance of those instructions he made an arrangement with an eminent firm of builders on the Clyde for a composite screw-steamer. The vessel was nearly ready for sea, but was still in possession of the builder, and was in fact their property, when she was seized by the Government."[139] The case did not go to trial. The owners came to a compromise with the government.

Confederate agents despaired of any success in obtaining cruisers or iron-clads in England, and they transferred their endeavors to France. The policy of England was based on expediency rather than on international law.[140] The chance of war with the United States was too great, and the inevitable consequences of such a war on Great Britain's commerce were too far reaching for her to take the risk. The occasion also provided England an opportunity to curtail neutral maritime rights. As a leading maritime power, it was to England's advantage to establish precedents which would be favorable to her as a belligerent nation. The prospect of American made iron-clads turned loose against her commerce was not a pleasant prospect to anticipate.

Confederate navy agents were not sent to France early in the war because of the nature of the Proclamation of Neutrality issued by the Emperor, Napoleon III, on June 10, 1861, which was very emphatic and specific. Among other prohibitions it "forbad any French subject to coöperate in any manner whatever in the equipment or armament of a vessel-of-war or a privateer for either belligerent."[141] The autocratic nature of the French government indicated that everything would depend upon the secret purposes of the Emperor. Confederate officials anticipated more freedom of action, a cheaper market, and more certain evidence of the attitude of the government in England. As the war

[139] *Ibid.*, II, 272 ff.
[140] See Owsley, *King Cotton Diplomacy*, chap. xiii for an explanation of British policy.
[141] Bulloch, *op. cit.*, II, 21.

progressed and England's attitude became such as to fore-stall the work of the Confederate navy agents, the prospect that the work might be carried on in France became brighter.

John Slidell had been permitted to communicate freely with the Emperor and the Ministers of State, and his oppor-tunity for obtaining authoritative information was considered excellent. Any policy which the Emperor espoused was un-doubtedly colored by his dream of an Empire in Mexico. Manifestly, Southern Independence would work to the ad-vantage of Imperialistic designs in Mexico.

Intimations that the Confederacy might achieve success in a ship building program in France reached Slidell in 1862. He obtained an interview with the Emperor on October 28, of that year, in which the Emperor led him to believe that a naval program in France was possible.[142]   At that time, Bulloch's financial resources were tied up in building projects in England. Slidell continued his investigations in France so that he might act when the time came. Napoleon's "pri-vate secretary and confidential friend," Mocquard, reported to him on January 4, 1863, that his majesty could not en-courage a shipbuilding program "for the present, at least."[143] But a few days later he was visited by Mr. Arman, "a mem-ber of the Corps Législatif and the largest shipbuilder in France,"[144] who offered to build iron-clad steamers for the Confederacy. He insisted that he spoke with authority, and Slidell was convinced that he made the offer at the Em-peror's suggestion.[145]

At the suggestion of D. de Lhuys, who promised to close his eyes as long as possible, Slidell went to Mr. Rouher, the minister of commerce, for "distinct assurance that if we were to build ships of war in French ports we should be permitted

[142] O. R. N., ser. II, vol. III, pp. 572-78 (memorandum of Slidell's inter-view as reported to Benjamin, October 28, 1862); Pickett Papers, Slidell to Benjamin, No. 19 (see enclosure); Bulloch, op. cit., II, 23 ff.
[143] O. R. N., ser. II, vol. III, pp. 638-39, Slidell to Benjamin, January 11, 1863.
[144] Ibid., p. 639.
[145] Ibid.

to arm and equip them and proceed to sea. This assurance was given by him. . . ."[146]

By this time the improbability of getting the iron-clads out of England was apparent. Bulloch was notified to transfer his work to France, and McRae was authorized to finance the project out of the Erlanger Loan.[147] Mallory was anxious to have at least four more ships similar to the "Alabama." In April, 1863, tentative contracts were signed with M. Arman and M. J. Voruz for four clipper corvettes.[148] Congress, by secret act, appropriated £2,000,000 for the construction of iron-clads in Southern Europe, and in June, Bulloch closed a contract with Arman for two powerful steam iron-clad rams.[149]

For some months the construction of the four corvettes and the two iron-clads progressed satisfactorily. But a series of events during the fall of 1863 and winter of 1864 changed the whole outlook.

In September, 1863, Bigelow and Dayton uncovered the secrets of the Confederate ship-building program. In October, England seized the Laird rams. In February, 1864, Napoleon refused to intervene in behalf of Mr. Bravay and the Laird rams. As early as November, 1863, Bulloch decided that the policy of France was one of deception.[150] As a matter of fact, Napoleon withered before the fire of the United States authorities. Secretary Seward made it plain to France that action in regard to the ships in question would be the test of friendship.[151] Bulloch wrote Mallory on February 18, 1864, that the policy of the Emperor was pronounced sooner than he had anticipated, and that the Emperor "has formally notified the builders that the ironclads

---

[146] *Ibid.*, p. 706, March 4, 1863, Slidell to Benjamin, March 4, 1863.

[147] *Ibid.*, II, 403 ff., Bulloch to North, April 13, 1863; III, 728-29, Benjamin to Mason, March 27, 1863; Pickett Papers, Benjamin to Mason, March 27, 1863; Bulloch, *op. cit.*, II, 25 ff.

[148] *Ibid.*, pp. 28 ff.; O. R. N., ser. II, vol. II, p. 431, Arman to Minister of the Marine and Colonies, June 1, 1863.

[149] *Ibid.*, pp. 464-66 (contract between Arman and Bulloch, July 16, 1863).

[150] Bulloch, *op. cit.*, II, 42.   [151] Bigelow, *op. cit.*, p. 34.

can not be permitted to sail, and that the corvettes must not be armed in France, but must be nominally sold to some foreign merchant and dispatched as ordinary trading vessels."[152]

Bulloch and Arman attempted to overcome the difficulty by fictitious sales to other parties. But on June 9, 1864, Bulloch was notified that Arman had disposed of the rams and corvettes "in obedience to the imperative orders of his government."[153]   Seward had intimidated Napoleon, as he had previously intimidated Lord Russell.[154]

Bulloch declared that "every pledge has been violated, and we have encountered nothing but deception and duplicity and are now their victims."[155]   Caleb Huse believed that Napoleon was "only a puppet in the hands of the Priests throughout the whole matter, Mexico and all."[156]

One of the iron-clads, the "Stonewall" ("Sphinx") was refused by Denmark and finally in January, 1865, successfully passed into the hands of the Confederacy. It has been suggested that in another month of war the "Stonewall" would have possession of Port Royal and that in two months the city of New York would probably have lain at her mercy.[157]   The efforts of the Confederate agents to build a navy in England and France ended with this French episode —a most disappointing termination of a program which promised so much for the Confederacy.

The naval agents under Bulloch's direction played an important rôle in the launching of a plan adopted in 1864 which provided for Government participation and control of blockade running. Steamers for the enterprise were to be selected by the naval agents and were to be under the control of the Navy Department. By September, 1864, Bulloch

[152] *O. R. N.*, ser. II, vol. II, p. 588.
[153] *Ibid.*, p. 667, Bulloch to Mallory, June 10, 1864.   The vessels were sold to Denmark and Prussia.
[154] Bigelow, *op. cit.*; John Bigelow, *Retrospections of an Active Life*, vols. I and II; Bulloch, *op. cit.*, vols. I and II; Owsley, *King Cotton Diplomacy* gives the details of this story.
[155] *O. R. N.*, ser. II, vol. II, p. 698, Bulloch to Mallory, August 5, 1864.
[156] Bigelow, *Retrospections*, II, 542-55, Huse to Bigelow, October 11, 1888.
[157] Bigelow, *France and the Confederate Navy*, p. 195.

had purchased four paddle steamers, the "Owl," "Bat," "Stag," and the "Deer," and had ten other steamers under construction.[158] The ships under construction were the "finest steamers that can be built for the special purpose of blockade running."[159] Bulloch also signed a contract in September for six torpedo boats.[160]

A half dozen of these blockade runners reached the Confederacy in time to make one or more trips through the blockade, two or three more were en route, and the remainder were not completed at the close of the war.[161] Some of the blockade runners were designed to serve the alternate purpose of making hostile marine raids.[162]

Needless to say, the private contractors accomplished little for the Navy Department. As a rule these individuals had no technical knowledge of such items as cost, structure, or the time necessary to build ships-of-war. They did not foresee the influence of the Foreign Enlistment Act, and other obstacles to be overcome in getting the ships out of England.[163]

Purchasing agents of the War and Navy Departments played a conspicuous rôle in blockade running enterprises. They had direct and indirect interests in blockade-running.

It has already been mentioned that James D. Bulloch was in command of the "Fingal" on her epoch making evasion of the blockade at Savannah early in November, 1861. The value of this precious cargo to the army covering Richmond can hardly be overestimated. It had been Bulloch's plan to carry the "Fingal" back to England for another cargo of munitions, but necessary delay of the ship at Savannah forced him to abandon the project in favor of

[158] O. R. N., ser. II, vol. II, pp. 720-22, Bulloch to Mallory, September 15, 1864.
[159] Ibid., p. 722.
[160] Ibid., p. 724, Bulloch to Mallory, September 16, 1864.
[161] Ibid., pp. 723-821; Bulloch, op. cit., II, 243.
[162] O. R. N., ser. II, vol. II, p. 723-24, Bulloch to Mallory, September 16, 1864.
[163] Bulloch, op. cit., II, 247.

another officer.[164] Bulloch was responsible for the purchase of the twin-screw steamer, "Coquette," for special duty as a blockade runner in 1863.[165]

The immediate reason for the purchase of the "Coquette" was to carry marine engines into the Confederacy. Lieutenant R. R. Carter was placed in command, and under his capable management the ship paid for herself many times over by running the blockade with war and navy supplies and by carrying out cotton to the sea islands.[166] Lieutenant Carter returned to England in 1864 to assist Bulloch in the purchase and construction of more blockade runners for the government. It has already been noted that several of these blockade-runners reached the Confederacy in time to see active service before the end of the war.[167]

The entrance of the Ordnance Bureau of the War Department into the blockade running business in 1863 was a significant forward step. From January to September, 1863, the ships purchased by Huse and Gorgas made twenty-two round trips through the blockade without a single capture.[168] The ships saved the Confederacy thousands of dollars in freight during these months alone. Caleb Huse constantly referred to the facility with which vessels eluded the blockade of Wilmington and Charleston in 1863.[169] The Confederate Government eventually decided to increase its profits by entering the lucrative trade on a large scale, prompted in part by the singular success of her purchasing agents in running the blockade.

Upon the shoulders of Bulloch and Huse fell the responsibility of shipping supplies from England and France. They selected the ships, government or private, on which the supplies were transported. More than once they decided upon the route which a vessel would take to a Confederate

[164] O. R. N., ser. II, vol. II, pp. 127-33.
[165] Ibid., pp. 511, 568-69; Bulloch, op. cit., II, 233 ff.
[166] O. R. N., ser. II, vol. II, pp. 568, 578, 594, 614, 702 ff.
[167] Bulloch, op. cit., II, 237-43.
[168] Pickett Papers, Benjamin to Slidell, August 29, 1863.
[169] Pickett Papers, Slidell to Benjamin, No. 28.

port. Shipping the supplies called for more painstaking effort than the actual purchase. After the capture of the sailing vessel, "Stephen Hart," early in the war, shipments were confined to steamers.[170] Most of the supplies, however, were shipped to the Sea Islands by the agents in Europe and from this point trans-shipped through the blockade by C. J. Helm, L. Heyliger, or N. S. Walker. They were intrusted with the meticulous details of blockade-running. They selected ships and pilots, and supervised the loading and the financial arrangements necessary for such an enterprise.[171]

Ships selected for blockade running were of "light draught and great speed. . . . Some of these steamers had been private yachts; some were engaged in trade between British ports, . . . [or] between England and France; . . . and some were built for opium smuggling in China."[172] Finally, there were ships constructed for the express purpose of running the American Blockade. Pilots were selected for their skill and daring, several of whom had been United States Navy officers preceding the war.[173]

Captures were so infrequent during the first years that the army was supplied with more arms, munitions, clothing, medicine, and such articles than has been generally suspected. "Europe furnished the Confederacy with its best ordnance, best muskets, best ammunition, and nearly all its uniforms."[174] Blockade running became one of the most lucrative of enterprises. It became a regular business, and continued so until the ports of the Confederacy were actually captured. By September, 1861, most of the stocks of Southern merchants were exhausted, and they were forced to obtain supplies from Europe.[175]

The blockade for many months was not even a respecta-

[170] Huse, *op. cit.*, p. 24.

[171] *O. R. N.*, ser. II, vols. II and III, see each name in index; Bulloch, *op. cit.*, vol. II, chap. iv; Mason Papers, especially vol. VI; Pickett Papers, Package 48; official dispatches.

[172] Huse, *op. cit.*, p. 25.   [173] *Ibid.*

[174] Willis, *op. cit.*, No. 257. (Manuscript Division, Library of Congress).
[175] *Ibid.*

ble paper blockade. The United States Navy had available for immediate service only three steamers when the blockade was declared.[176] There were only forty steamers in the Navy, and they were scattered abroad. Even with this total and with many more additional ships, the task of blockading an irregular coastline of 3500 miles with its innumerable rivers, inlets, and interior channels of every description appears ridiculous. "An effective blockade on such a scale was a thing unprecedented, even in the operation of the foremost naval power of the world."[177] The United States was not a party to the Treaty of Paris, but its rule in regard to a blockade was generally recognized, that is, "Blockades, to be binding, must be effective—that is to say, maintained by a force sufficient really to prevent access to the coast of the enemy."[178] Reports of American, British, and French consuls agree with those of Confederate agents and other officials that the blockade preceding the spring of 1862 was ineffective.[179] It was in 1863 that the blockade runners of the Ordnance Department launched upon their successful career. Of the vessels operating out of Nassau from January, 1863, to April, 1864, only one out of six was reported captured.[180]

The Confederate agents at Nassau and Bermuda performed a valuable piece of work by keeping a record of blockade violations and forwarding the material to their officials. Henry Hotze used these statistics in his English publication, the *Index*, which in turn helped to build up the blockade running business.[181]

It is impossible to estimate accurately the value of the goods which passed through the blockade. Edward Willis, on the staff of General Beauregard during the war, and at

---

[176] Soley, *op. cit.*, p. 26.

[177] *Ibid.*, p. 27. For detailed discussion of the blockade see Owsley, *King Cotton Diplomacy*, chap. viii; Soley, *op. cit.*; Willis, *op. cit.*; Brandlee, *op. cit.*; Official Records, Blockade Runners; Pickett Papers, Reports of Agents; Mason Papers.

[178] Soley, *op. cit.*, p. 26.

[179] Owsley, *King Cotton Diplomacy*, pp. 256 ff.

[180] *Ibid.*, p. 274.   [181] *Ibid.*, pp. 273 ff.

the same time confidential clerk of John Fraser and Company, estimated it at $200,000,000.[182] Fraser and Company was the commercial king of the South in war time. This firm bought nearly all the blockade goods which were run into Charleston. Major Willis in turn bought them for the Confederacy.[183] He made one purchase in 1863 amounting to $7,500,000.[184] If a vessel made two successful trips through the blockade, she paid for herself and made a handsome profit. "When half-crowns could be turned into sovereigns at a single venture, capitalists could afford to run almost any risk."[185] The foreign commerce of Wilmington in 1863 was four times as much as all of the ports of North Carolina in 1858.[186] It was estimated that Charleston did an annual foreign commerce of $21,600,000 in 1863.[187] Fifteen thousand bales of cotton were shipped from Charleston and Wilmington during April and May, 1863.[188]

Data of the above sort could be continued at length. Of greater consequence for this study is an estimate of the amount and value of munitions which passed through the blockade into the Confederacy. Again the record is somewhat confusing. From September 30, 1862, to September 20, 1863, the steamers of the Ordnance Bureau alone imported 113,504 small arms besides five rifled Blakely guns and other supplies. From the available records Huse imported approximately 350,000 stands of small arms. Of this total there were 100,000 Austrian rifles, a few Brunswick rifles and . revolvers, some 25,000 British muskets and the balance Enfield rifles. All of the above were first class arms, and the Enfield rifles had no superior. It is probable that the various agents, official, state, and private, succeeded in running a half million or more small arms through the blockade.[189] This estimate is based on the assumption that the

[182] Willis, *op. cit.*   [183] *Ibid.*   [184] *Ibid.*
[185] Soley, *op. cit.*, p. 155.
[186] Pickett Papers, Benjamin to Slidell, No. 23.
[187] *Ibid.*   [188] *Ibid.*
[189] *O. R.*, ser. IV, vol. I, pp. 957-59; II, 52, 227, 382-84, 955-58; III, 733, 928-30, 986-88; *ibid.*, ser. I, vol. XXXIV, pt. iv, p. 666; Bulloch, *op. cit.*, vols. I and II; Huse, *op. cit.*; Schwab, *op. cit.*

records are practically complete. It is probable, however, that those for 1864 are incomplete. This calculation does not take into account powder, cannon, cartridges, cavalry sabers, leather, shoes, boots, cloth, socks, flannel, and sundry supplies.

Huse spent approximately six millions of dollars during the first eighteen months in Europe.[190] It is impossible to obtain an accurate figure for his disbursements during the last two years, but it is probable that he did not spend that much. The report of Fraser, Trenholm and Company as of December 7, 1864, lists drafts drawn against them by Caleb Huse totaling £801,913—approximately four millions of dollars.[191] A few months earlier, Huse had secured £40,000 credit from J. K. Gilliat and Company for supplies in France, a sum which does not seem to be included in the above statement.[192] Huse continued to purchase and forward supplies even in the fall of 1864 at a remarkable pace. His drafts on Fraser, Trenholm and Company during the month of October total $875,000.[193] Fraser, Trenholm and Company lists drafts by other agents totaling approximately two and one quarter millions of dollars outstanding in December, 1864.[194] Available figures for the amount spent by the agents of the War Department total, therefore, approximately twelve and a quarter millions of dollars. This is twice as much as was realized from the Erlanger Loan.

The Naval agents were able to complete few contracts for ships. The cost of the "Alabama," "Florida," and the "Shenandoah" including their cruises totaled approximately $900,000.[195] The six steamers which Bulloch contracted for in 1864 were to cost about $700,000.[196] Available figures indicate that Bulloch spent at least two and one-half millions

---

[190] *O. R.*, ser. IV, vol. II, pp. 382-84 (memorandum of Gorgas, February 3, 1863).

[191] Trenholm Papers, portfolio I, December 7, 1864.

[192] *O. R.*, ser. IV, vol. III, pp. 525-29, McRae to Seddon, July 4, 1864.

[193] Trenholm Papers, portfolio I, October, 1864.

[194] *Ibid.*   [195] Bulloch, *op. cit.*, II, 275.

[196] *O. R.*, ser. IV, vol. III, pp. 525-29, McRae to Seddon, July 4, 1864.

of dollars.[197] Congress voted at one time $10,000,000 for the Navy Department, but it was one thing to vote credit, and another to make it available for the agents.

It was the lack of credit rather than the dangers of the blockade which limited the purchase and shipment of supplies by the purchasing agents. It is probable that eighty per cent of all the supplies shipped by the agents reached the Confederate States.[198]

---

[197] Trenholm Papers, portfolio I.

[198] This is based on the assumption that goods shipped by the agents evaded the blockade in proportion to the total evasions. See Owsley, *King Cotton Diplomacy*, chap. viii.

CHAPTER III

FINANCIAL EXPERIMENTS

THE WORK of the agents and the effectiveness of their operations were determined in a large measure by the general financial policy of the Confederacy. Political and international considerations played a major rôle in determining the financial policy of the Confederacy both at home and abroad. It is probable that her statesmen erred more in political than in economic insight. She secured about twenty-seven millions of dollars in specie during the course of the war; yet, she managed to spend hundreds of millions of dollars.[1] By an interesting turn of fate, the very principle for which she was fighting—that of State Rights—proved to be a most serious obstacle in the way of a successful financial program. Blocked by the individual states in moves toward direct taxation, and cut off from export and import revenues by the Federal blockade, the Confederacy was forced to depend almost entirely upon treasury notes and bond issues to meet current expenses.

One of the first questions which faced the men who organized the Confederacy at Montgomery on the eighth of February, 1861, was, "What shall we use for money?" The answer to this question involves a story which begins with the search for a skilled engraver, and ends four years later with a nation flooded with depreciated notes and bonds. The Confederacy might have avoided financial bankruptcy had all her officials realized that four years of struggle faced them, and that the Federal blockade would never be broken by European powers. She has been severely criticized for her financial policy, but seldom has that criticism been leveled at the vital points of weakness. The causes of the financial col-

[1] Schwab, *op. cit.*, p. 36.

lapse lie deeper than the failure to tax, or the over-issue of currency, or bonds. These were simply the inevitable expressions of certain beliefs which were current in the Confederate States. Military defeat and financial collapse were simultaneous, and it is erroneous to place the blame at any one point.

The South might rely on the patriotic spirit of her citizens to insure the success of bond issues at home. Promises to pay in the form of Treasury notes might circulate as money. Even taxation and impressment might be resorted to as a final desperate policy. But, the last year of the war was financed largely by creating a huge floating debt amounting to hundreds of millions of dollars.[2]

During the years of financial chaos at home, the purchasing agents abroad felt the pinch of limited finances. Their activities were limited from the beginning by lack of money. The agents soon discovered that European business men were eager for cash or its equivalent.

During the first eighteen months of the war the agents abroad were financed chiefly by the use of letters of credit or Treasury warrants, and bills of exchange. Gold was shipped as rapidly as possible to Fraser, Trenholm and Company in Liverpool, against which letters of credit were issued. Bills of exchange were purchased from Southern banks and business firms with Confederate money, and these houses would ship gold or cotton abroad to meet the bills.[3] The rate of exchange mounted rapidly, and soon became prohibitive. On January 24, 1862, gold was selling at twenty-five per cent premium. By October, of the same year, sterling was worth 150% premium, and from that time on the premium rose rapidly to 1000% by October, 1863.[4]

Banks and commercial houses subscribed liberally to the first Confederate loan of fifteen million on February 28,

[2] *Ibid.*, p. 83.
[3] *O. R.*, ser. IV, vol. I, pp. 343-45, 538-42, 1007-8, 1115; II, 236-37.
[4] Pickett Papers, Slidell to Benjamin, No. 47; Mason Papers, V, 989; *ibid.*, III, 643.

1861, and thus lost much of their specie at the outset of the war. Eight millions were subscribed by July, 1861. "Of the entire amount two-fifths were subscribed in New Orleans, less than one-fourth in South Carolina, less than one-tenth each in Virginia and Alabama."[5]

Most of the specie which was shipped abroad by the Confederacy was secured from this loan. By September 30, 1861, some $1,400,000 had been sent to Huse to buy supplies.[6] During January, February, and March of 1862, $1,261,600 was shipped to Fraser, Trenholm and Company and placed to his credit.[7] Limited amounts of coin and specie were shipped throughout the war,[8] but this method of financing the agents was limited almost entirely to the first eighteen months.

By the fall of 1862, the resources at the command of the agents in Europe were so limited that their credit was endangered. Huse had purchased twice as much as he could pay for, and Isaac, Campbell and Company was pressing payment.[9] The other agents were forced to remain inactive for lack of funds. It was imperative that credit be established at the earliest possible moment. The produce loan, so-called Hundred Million Dollar Loan, because it was increased to that amount on August 19, 1861, was subscribed almost entirely in cotton. By the end of 1861, 400,000 bales of cotton had been offered.[10] The price of cotton rose rapidly in Europe during 1862,[11] and the probability of using cotton to raise funds appealed to numerous officials about the same time.

It was one thing to agree on the use of cotton to raise money but another thing to find a practical method of mak-

---

[5] Schwab, *op. cit.*, p. 8.

[6] *O. R.*, ser. IV, vol. I, pp. 564-65, 594, 596, 633.

[7] *Ibid.*, pp. 985 (Benjamin to Huse, March 10, 1862), 1007 (Benjamin to Isaac, Campbell and Co.).

[8] Trenholm Papers, portfolio I.

[9] *O. R.*, ser. IV, vol. II, p. 227, Gorgas to Seddon, December 5, 1862; also pp. 190-91, Hart to Randolph, November 17, 1862. Huse had been furnished with $3,095,139.18 and still owed £444,850 ($5,925,402).

[10] Schwab, *op. cit.*, p. 13.   [11] To about fifty cents per pound.

ing the funds available for use in Europe. The Confederate Government had no boats for carrying out the cotton. Even the Ordnance Bureau had not at this time established its line of steamers. Blockade-running had been encouraged in the hope of creating sentiment in Europe against the blockade, but the business was still in private hands. By an embargo on cotton, and by proving the ineffectiveness of the blockade, the Confederacy hoped to precipitate foreign intervention. This policy was explained by Slidell when he wrote to Benjamin at a later date, "So long as we had any reason to hope that practical illustrations of the inefficiency of the blockade might lead to a denial by European powers of its obligatory force it was wise to hold out every inducement to individual enterprise to multiply those illustrations."[12]

In keeping with this illusion, and in the absence of a government fleet of blockade runners, several methods of utilizing the cotton were suggested. Early in 1862 Benjamin suggested to a representative of an European banking house, then stationed at New Orleans, that cotton be deposited in the hands of the bank's agent as collateral for an advance of a million dollar loan to be deposited in England.[13] This plan failed to materialize before New Orleans fell into the hands of the enemy. Confederate officials apparently could not agree, or could not formulate a practical plan. Gorgas was determined to supply Huse with funds and in the absence of any other method dispatched N. S. Walker with $2,000,-000 in Confederate bonds to deposit with Huse.[14]

In the summer of the same year, Stephen D. Mallory, who was equally as anxious as Gorgas to supply his department with funds, dispatched G. N. Sanders to Europe with authority to use cotton certificates for the construction of ships. The method which Mallory had in mind was to have Sanders contract for ships payable in cotton delivered at any

[12] Pickett Papers, No. 59, Slidell to Benjamin, April 7, 1864.
[13] O. R., ser. IV, vol. I, pp. 845-46, Benjamin to Forstall, January 17, 1862.
[14] Ibid., II, 227, Gorgas to Seddon, December 5, 1862.

port in possession of the Confederate States, at the price current at the time of delivery.[15]

William Lindsay and Company in England advised Sanders and Mason that it approved of a plan to hypothecate cotton, but such cotton bonds or certificates could not be negotiated unless a definite price for the cotton was set.[16] Lindsay suggested that the price be fixed at four pence and expressed his willingness to negotiate on these terms. As the Sanders contract was exceptionally large, Mason refused to take the responsibility for making the change and dispatched Sanders back to the Confederacy to adjust the difficulty.[17] Mason approved of the idea and wrote Benjamin on September 18, 1862, "I have every reason to believe from four to five million sterling or more if required, could be commanded in this form from the cotton spinners alone."[18]

In the meantime, George T. Sinclair had arrived in England with orders to purchase or build a ship for the Navy Department, "under instructions that funds would be supplied him for the purpose out of means placed in the hands of Captain Bulloch."[19] But these funds were exhausted. Sinclair appealed to Mason, and he took the responsibility for furnishing Sinclair with £62,000 of cotton bonds at eight cents per pound. The Government endorsed Mason's approval of the Sinclair bonds,[20] which were the first cotton bonds used by the agents in Europe.[21] The Treasury Department had printed by this time thousands of dollars worth of cotton certificates secured by the cotton of the produce loan.

With Mason's approval of the type of bond suggested by

<hr />

[15] Mason Papers, Mason to Benjamin, No. 16, September 18, 1862.

[16] Ibid.

[17] Ibid., Mason to Mallory, September 18, 1862.

[18] Ibid., Mason to Benjamin, No. 16, September 18, 1862.

[19] Ibid.

[20] Ibid., Mason to Benjamin, No. 25, January 14, 1863, acknowledges the approval.

[21] Copy of the Sinclair Cotton Bond, called a cotton certificate is found in ibid., Mason to Benjamin, No. 19, November 4, 1862.

Lindsay and Company, and under the extreme necessity of making funds available for the agents in Europe, President Davis, Memminger, and Benjamin agreed to carry out the plan. Mason had also recommended James Spence for the position of financial agent abroad, insisting that it "would be a well merited recompense to Mr. Spence for his persistent and valuable labors in our cause."[22] To this suggestion Benjamin responded favorably, but instead of notifying Spence of his appointment, he wrote directly to Mason, and in the dispatch of October 28, it is intimated that Spence would have a part in supervising the cotton loans.[23] Vague statements which Benjamin made from time to time probably led Spence to assume greater responsibilities than it was ever intended that he should.

The permission to use cotton certificates or bonds in Europe opened up immense possibilities, but there were many dangers attached to a haphazard use of them. Commander Maury was dispatched to England by Secretary Mallory, "to obtain money for the naval purposes committed to his charge, by means of such cotton obligations, should he find it necessary and practicable. He brought a like authority to other naval officers here who had actual contracts in course of execution for building ships."[24] If each department should pursue an independent policy, the agents would become competitors, and bonds would be dumped wholesale on the market. Mason suggested and Spence agreed that the agents should meet and determine a systematic policy of paying for supplies.[25]

The rising price of cotton in Europe and the rumor that the Confederacy would use cotton bonds to finance their

[22] Pickett Papers, Mason to Benjamin, No. 9, 1862.
[23] Ibid., Benjamin to Mason, No. 8, October 28, 1862. James Spence, an English subject and friend of Mason, was a financier and talented writer. In 1861 he published the American Union; and proved himself a resourceful and energetic friend of the Confederacy. For material on Spence, see Mason Papers, vols. III-V; Pickett Papers and Official Records (especially O. R. N., ser. II, vol. III); Owsley, King Cotton Diplomacy.
[24] Pickett Papers, Mason to Benjamin, No. 22, December 10, 1862.
[25] Mason Papers, IV, 724, Spence to Mason, December 31, 1862.

agents created a stir in speculative circles. A representative of Isaac, Campbell and Company offered a contract to supply 100,000 men; and accept a substantial payment in cotton certificates.[26] Lieutenant North had word from merchants in Glasgow that cotton certificates could be marketed there.[27] Lindsay and Company offered to issue cotton bonds at regular intervals and prove its good faith by purchasing two and a half million of dollars of them for its own account.[28] Confederate officials in France were approached by French bankers with offers to float loans.[29] The individual states of the Confederacy took steps to negotiate for the sale of cotton and bonds in Europe and to purchase supplies with the funds.[30]

While Mason and Spence were seeking permission from Richmond to use cotton certificates, Slidell and Huse were negotiating with a French banking house, Erlanger and Company, for a bond issue. It was just at this time that intimations were made to Slidell that naval operations in France might be satisfactorily carried on. Even the Emperor had given him some encouragement. There was a political prize of tremendous importance at stake. Slidell was convinced of Erlanger's political importance and believed that in the event of a successful contract with them that the "very strongest influences,"[31] would be enlisted in favor of the Confederacy. Slidell and Huse drew up a tentative contract with them to dispose of £5,000,000 in Confederate cotton bonds bearing eight per cent.[32] The terms agreed to by Huse and Slidell were most exacting, but the supposed diplomatic advantage to be gained either stupefied

[26] Pickett Papers, Hart to Benjamin, November 17, 1862.
[27] Mason Papers, IV, 861, North to Mason, February 19, 1863.
[28] Pickett Papers, Mason to Benjamin, No. 19, November 4, 1862.
[29] *Ibid.*, De Leon to Benjamin, No. 1 and 2; *ibid.*, Slidell to Benjamin, No. 18.
[30] Mason Papers, III, 671, November 1, 1862.
[31] Pickett Papers, Slidell to Benjamin, No. 18.
[32] Mason Papers, III, 648 ff, copy of the contract containing twenty-two articles.

their business sense, or induced them to make a tremendous sacrifice.[33]

Mason was not so intrigued with Erlanger's political importance and felt that he could not append his signature to the tentative contract. Lindsay and Company had outlined a proposition which he preferred to the Erlanger contract. But, Mason would not oppose the scheme in view of Slidell's insistence on it as a political device.[34] The proposition suggested by Lindsay on the advice of his stockbroker was similar to the plan which had already been experimented with in the case of George T. Sinclair.[35] Lindsay proposed that the legislature pass a law authorizing the issue of sterling bonds, represented by bales of New Orleans middling cotton. The bond would entitle the holder to demand a certain number of bales of cotton at one of the Confederate ports, either during the war or within twelve months after. If the cotton was not claimed within the prescribed time, the bonds were to be considered as sterling bonds, and, on demand coupons given, payable at the seat of government at a specified rate. It was recommended that the price of cotton be fixed at four pence per pound, which was considerably less than the average price for the seven years preceding the war. Lindsay believed that such bonds if issued in small installments at first would command a premium and the Government would enjoy the prestige and benefit of such increased price.[36]

Benjamin and Memminger had several conferences on the Lindsay and Erlanger proposals. As to the Lindsay offer, it was Benjamin's opinion that the services of Lindsay and Company might be quite acceptable providing the government wished to float a foreign loan, which was not the case. Moreover, Spence had been sent a batch of cotton cer-

[33] *Ibid.*, Erlanger was to get all above 70% on the bonds, a 5% commission on the sales and a 1% commission on the sinking funds.

[34] Pickett Papers, Mason to Benjamin, No. 19, November 4, 1862.

[35] *Ibid.*, for copy of Lindsay's proposition and copy of the Sinclair cotton certificate.

[36] *Ibid.*, Mason to Benjamin, No. 19, with enclosures.

tificates based on cotton at five pence per pound, which rate was considered excessively low, and they were sent only with the hope that they would command a handsome premium. It was not considered expedient, therefore, to float a loan with Lindsay and Company.[37]

The Erlanger agents arrived in Richmond a few days before Mason's dispatches explaining their mission and the great importance which Slidell attached to the scheme. Consequently their contract was rejected. On the arrival of Mason's dispatches, the government reconsidered the plan and finally agreed to take £3,000,000 instead of £5,000,000 which had been offered. More liberal terms were secured. Erlanger agreed to give 77% for the bonds instead of 70%. The interest rate was reduced from eight to seven per cent, and in case the bonds were redeemed in cotton six pence per pound would be allowed. Benjamin stated that the contract would have been declined altogether, "but for the political considerations indicated by Mr. Slidell, in whose judgment in such matters we are disposed to place very great confidence."[38]

While these negotiations were in progress at Richmond, the purchasing agents were at a loss as to a method of meeting their obligations and making new contracts. Large remittances of Confederate bonds and cotton certificates had been made by the several departments to their respective agents in Europe. Upon inquiry Spence found that the Confederate bonds could not be used at better rates than fifty cents on the dollar, and they were withheld.[39] This was probably due to the increased rate of interest in England which had risen from three to five per cent during January, 1863. Further advances were expected. Lead in this action was taken by the Bank of England.[40]

Mason in consultation with other officials and agents

[37] *Ibid.*, Benjamin to Mason, No. 12, January 15, 1863.
[38] *Ibid.*
[39] *Ibid.*, Mason to Benjamin, No. 32, March 30, 1863.
[40] *Ibid.*, Mason to Benjamin, No. 29, February 5, 1863.

deemed it judicious to withhold the cotton certificates from the market until he could learn the result of the proposals for a direct loan.[41]   However, Huse and the other agents were reminded constantly of the urgent necessity of shipping supplies as rapidly as possible.   War department orders and dispatches had Huse in a frenzy.[42]   In the emergency Mason authorized him to issue cotton warrants calling for the delivery of 5,000,000 pounds of cotton at five pence sterling per pound "as payment pro tanto of indebtedness"[43] for supplies already purchased from Isaac, Campbell and Company and shipped to the War Department.   Huse was also authorized to contract for the delivery of 2,300,000 pounds of cotton in payment of additional supplies.[44]   Mason also endorsed for Captain Maury, about the same time, 500 certificates for twenty bales of cotton of five hundred pounds each, deliverable at New Orleans or Mobile, which had been issued at the Treasury of the Confederate States under the date of November 1, 1862.[45]   On March 11, 1863, Mason signed three hundred additional certificates like the ones mentioned above, to be used by the navy agents.[46]   Thus, 15,300,000 pounds of cotton were pledged by agents in Europe as an emergency measure while waiting for the outcome of a direct loan.   This does not include the £60,000 sterling which had been raised on cotton certificates for Sinclair in 1862.

Rumors reached Europe early in February that Erlanger's agents had reached an agreement with the Confederacy for a loan, but that the amount was considerably smaller than had been anticipated.   This news was received with favor by Mason, Spence, and others who believed that prospective sales of cotton in the form of cotton certificates offered a more advantageous mode of raising money.[47]

[41] *Ibid.*, No. 29 and 32.
[42] Mason Papers, IV, 788, Huse to Mason, January 31, 1863.
[43] Pickett Papers, Mason to Benjamin, No. 29, February 5, 1863.
[44] *Ibid.*; see also No. 28, contract with M. Bellot.
[45] Mason Papers, IV, 857, February 18, 1863.   [46] *Ibid.*
[47] Pickett Papers, Mason to Benjamin, No. 29, February 23, 1863.

When the terms of the Erlanger Loan became known in Europe, James Spence, to whom the proposition had never appealed, insisted that the "volunteer bankers of the Confederacy had driven a very hard bargain," and that "far better terms could have been made with an old established banking house."[48] He considered the terms preposterous, and pledged himself to amend them as far as possible.[49] He sent Erlanger a plan for placing the loan before the public, a plan which would save the government thousands of dollars in interest.[50] Spence notified Erlanger before he had heard of the terms drawn up at Richmond that he would proceed without them unless a favorable plan could be worked out.[51]

Erlanger answered his letters in evasive and polite terms until he could confer with Slidell.[52] Slidell apparently knew nothing of the appointment of Spence as financial agent, and he considered this attempted supervision as pernicious meddling.[53] Spence seemed to anticipate future developments even more clearly than the astute Benjamin. Benjamin believed that the takers of the loan would reap immense profits but that the political advantage which Slidell had visioned would be speedily consummated.[54] Spence remained doubtful and continued to offer suggestions and amendments. Finally Erlanger and Slidell became exasperated. Erlanger notified Spence that they could proceed without his help, and Slidell complained bitterly to Mason of the Englishman who considered his personal interests invaded by the arrangement made at Richmond.[55]

When Erlanger and Company indicated in their correspondence with Spence that his suggestions were not acceptable, Spence decided to go to Paris. He wrote Mason,

[48] *Ibid.*, De Leon to Secretary of State, No. 6, February 23, 1863.
[49] Mason Papers, vol. IV, Spence to Mason, February 6, 1863.
[50] *Ibid.*
[51] *Ibid.*, IV, 741, January 12, 1863.
[52] *Ibid.*, p. 855, Spence to Mason, February 18, 1863.
[53] *Ibid.*, Slidell to Mason, February 15, 1863.
[54] Pickett Papers, Benjamin to Slidell, No. 11, January 15, 1863.
[55] Mason Papers, vol. IV, Slidell to Mason, February 15, 1863.

"After the care exercised for a number of months to avoid damage to this treaty it will be mortifying to be treated with something like polite contempt in return, and I am not the man to take it easily."[56] But the ideas of Erlanger and Slidell prevailed. Slidell represented the Confederate Government in France, and Spence could not question his sovereignty.

Spence had felt for some months that his duties as financial agent should be defined, and that the appointment should be attended with some formality. Memminger in answer to this request wrote Spence on February 9, 1863, "The Treasury Department of the Confederate States having full confidence in your ability and good conduct hereby appoint you its financial agent in Great Britain, to negotiate and carry out such arrangements for the raising and payment of money as it may from time to time require."[57] This dispatch did not reach Spence until the middle of March, only a few days before the Erlanger bonds were placed on the market.[58] Word also came from Richmond that General C. J. McRae, a man familiar with the cotton trade had been appointed as special agent for the Erlanger Loan.[59] These communications placed definite limits on Spence's authority and sphere, but he apparently did not object.[60]

Erlanger gradually won the esteem of Mason and the purchasing agents during the weeks before the loan was placed on the market. Attention has already been called to the extreme financial crisis which the agents faced during the months before the Erlanger contract arrived. When definite word reached the Erlanger offices that a contract had been signed with the Confederate States, Erlanger offered to advance sums wanted for the immediate necessities of the agents in Europe.[61] Thus, the existing inconvenience for

[56] Ibid., p. 855, Spence to Mason, February 18, 1863.
[57] Ibid., p. 833, February 9, 1863.
[58] Ibid., p. 908, March 17, 1863.
[59] Ibid., p. 823, February 7, 1863.
[60] Ibid., p. 908, Spence to Mason, March 17, 1863.
[61] Pickett Papers, Mason to Benjamin, No. 32.

lack of money was somewhat obviated. It was to the advantage of Erlanger as well as to the Confederate States that the cotton certificates be withheld from the market.

About the middle of March the official dispatches and a copy of the secret act of Congress authorizing the loan reached Europe. Some days before, Erlanger had secured the approval of the Emperor and of De Lhuys to advertise the loan. De Lhuys objected at first, stating that newspaper advertisements "would excite unfriendly comment and probably be made the subject of a protest from the Federal minister."[62] But the Emperor at Erlanger's request addressed a note to De Lhuys which led to a withdrawal of his objections. This fact further convinced Slidell of his Majesty's friendship.[63]

The prospectus of the loan was issued on March 18, and on March 19, the books were opened for subscriptions in the principal markets of England, France, Holland, and Germany, namely, Liverpool, London, Paris, Amsterdam, and Frankfort. J. H. Shroeder and Company were the London agents, and they received orders for £5,000,000 the first day,[64] almost twice the sum of the entire loan. The books were kept open two and one-half days, and the total subscriptions reached nearly £16,000,000, more than five times the authorized issue.[65]

Financial circles in London had freely prophesied that the enterprise was a hazardous one, and that it would likely fail in the market.[66] Its success surprised the most optimistic. Erlanger and the Confederate officials were overjoyed. Mason wrote Benjamin of the brilliant success of the loan, and congratulated him on the "triumphant success of our infant credit; it shows malgré all detraction and calumny, that cotton is King at last."[67] Hotze described it

<hr />

[62] *Ibid.*, Slidell to Benjamin, No. 28, March 4, 1863.
[63] *Ibid.*
[64] *Ibid.*, Mason to Benjamin, No. 31, March 20, 1863.
[65] *Ibid.*, Mason to Benjamin, No. 32, March 30, 1863.
[66] *Ibid.*, Mason to Benjamin, No. 31, March 20, 1863.
[67] *Ibid.*, No. 32.

as a moral victory and wrote Benjamin, "The organs of the Northern Government and the ultra section of the Exeter Hall school prove that they also feel it to be such by even more than usual vehemence in their denunciations of the 'infamous schemes of the hell-born rebel Confederacy.' "[68] Slidell wrote, "It is a financial recognition of our independence, emanating from a class proverbially cautious and little given to be influenced by sentiment or sympathy."[69]

The fact that the loan was over-subscribed five times gave them some reason to be enthusiastic. This gauge alone can not be taken as an accurate criterion of the demand for this type of bond. When subscribing for Government loans, it was the custom for subscribers to put their names down for three or four times more than they wanted, for such loans were usually over-subscribed several times. Allotments were based on the amount subscribed. If an individual wanted ten bonds, and he estimated that the loan would be over-subscribed three times, he would sign for thirty bonds.[70] This custom proved ruinous to many investors in the Mexican loan during the spring of 1864. News of the hostile attitude of the United States toward a monarchical government in Mexico, as expressed by H. W. Davis in a resolution to Congress, arrived in France during the middle of the subscriptions. Subscriptions for the Mexican loan immediately ceased and each subscriber was forced by France to take the full amount of his subscription.[71] Spence probably understood better than the Confederates this peculiarity of European finance, for his correspondence does not portray any exhilarant mood when the loan was over-subscribed.

Hotze and Mason pointed out to Benjamin that there were several new loans before the financial public, Danish, New Italian, Russian, Portuguese, and that the Portuguese was the only one, other than the Erlanger loan which was

---

[68] Pickett Papers, Hotze to Benjamin, No. 20, March 21, 1863.
[69] *Ibid.*, Slidell to Benjamin, No. 29, March 21, 1863.
[70] Bigelow, *France and the Confederate Navy*, pp. 39-42, Bigelow to Seward, May 3, 1864.
[71] *Ibid.*, p. 40.

selling at a premium.[72]   Several of the English newspapers were convinced that the loan was a success.   The *Post* said, "The terms of this loan appear so advantageous to the lenders, that we doubt not the sum asked for has at once been subscribed."[73]   The *Times* stated, "Very little political feeling has been manifested in the business, and it seems evident as far as London is concerned, that it is viewing it as cotton speculation."[74]   The *Herald* was more emphatic: "So great a success, under what may be considered comparatively doubtful circumstances, has not been witnessed for a lengthened period."[75]   The *London Economist* endorsed the loan and made this interesting comment, " 'It may appear somewhat startling that the Confederates should be able to borrow in Europe while the Federal Government has been unable to obtain a shilling from that usually liberal and enterprising quarter!' "[76]

The bonds were offered at 90, and sold at a 5% premium on the first day.[77]   Within a week speculative interest had somewhat lagged, and they were quoted at 92.[78]   In less than two weeks the bonds were quoted at 85 to 86.   This sudden drop alarmed Erlanger and Mason.   Erlanger insisted that agents of the Federal Government were making concerted efforts to discredit the loan by large purchases at low rates.[79]   This movement had encouraged the formation of a "bear" party which threatened to drive the bonds to the point that investors who had paid only 15% would forfeit their subscriptions before the next installment date.   McRae had not arrived in Europe; so Mason in consultation with Slidell, Erlanger, and Spence formulated a plan to sustain the market.[80]

[72] Pickett Papers, Hotze to Benjamin, No. 20, March 21, 1863; Mason to Benjamin, No. 32, March 30, 1863.
[73] *Ibid.*, Hotze to Benjamin, No. 20, enclosing clippings of various newspapers.
[74] *Ibid.*   [75] *Ibid.*
[76] Owsley, *King Cotton Diplomacy*, p. 400, quoted from "Economist."
[77] Pickett Papers, Hotze to Benjamin, No. 20; Mason to Benjamin, Nos. 31, 32, and 33.   [78] *Ibid.*   [79] *Ibid.*
[80] *Ibid.*, Mason to Benjamin, No. 33, April 9, 1863.

On April 7, Mason signed a secret agreement which authorized Erlanger to purchase bonds on account of Confederate Government up to an amount of 1,000,000 pounds sterling if necessary.[81] Again Spence found himself at variance with Mason and Slidell. Spence denounced Erlanger and Company for its attempt to place the blame for the depreciating trend of the bonds on a "bear" organization. He believed the loan was in the hands of an incompetent organization. The bonds were offered at 90, a price which was too high to be sustained even by well-organized European governments.[82] Spence suggested that a more effective expedient for bolstering the market would be the withdrawal of one-third of the bonds.[83] Erlanger's agents informed Spence that they had contracted to sell the bonds, and if the market was not sustained, the Confederate Government would lose the 15% which had been advanced by subscribers and that the whole plan would collapse.[84]

The use of Confederate funds to "bull" the market began on April 8, and within two days about £400,000 were used driving the bonds above par.[85] Purchases were continued during the following days to maintain them at the issue price. By April 24, the £1,000,000 allotted Erlanger had been spent, and Mason gave him permission to use £500,000 more if necessary.[86] With these funds the bonds were kept at par until the middle of May.[87] After this date they fluctuated somewhat, but did not change materially until the fall of Vicksburg.[88] Rumors which reached Europe in regard to the burning or capture of Southern cotton always had an adverse effect on the market price of the bonds.[89] Hotze explained that several other facts caused the loan to

---

[81] *Ibid.*, see enclosure for copy of the agreement.
[82] Mason Papers, vol. V, Spence to Mason, April 3 and 4, 1863.
[83] *Ibid.*, May 9, 1863.   [84] *Ibid.*
[85] Pickett Papers, Mason to Benjamin, April 27, 1863, (unofficial).
[86] For full account of the money spent see enclosures to Mason's letter to Benjamin, April 27.
[87] *Ibid.*, Mason to Benjamin, No. 36, May 11, 1863.
[88] *Ibid.*, Hotze to Benjamin, No. 27, August 27, 1863.
[89] *Ibid.*

fluctuate from time to time. Among these were, first, the suspension of the house of Spence Bros., of Liverpool, the leading partner of which was confounded by many with his brother, James Spence; second, rumors spread by Federal agents that the Confederacy was about to float another and larger loan; third, the impression that Erlanger and Company was allowed a very large margin of profit.[90]   In August, when the loan dropped to 36% discount, Hotze wrote Benjamin, "It is stated positively by those who have the means of knowing that large sums of money are being freely sacrificed to injure the credit of the Confederacy."[91]

Spence continued to place the major blame on Erlanger and Company. He believed the Confederacy had been tricked, and that Erlanger had benefitted most by the millions spent by Mason in the re-purchase of bonds.[92]   As a matter of fact, the Confederacy received only 68% on each bond. Erlanger and Company received all above 77 plus a five per cent commission for selling and a 1% commission as collecting agent. An annual sinking fund of 5% was established to retire the bonds. When it is considered that the Confederacy re-purchased one-half the subscription, leaving £1,500,000 in the hands of the public, the yield would be approximately $5,000,000. Redemption of the bonds began on March 1, 1864, at the rate of 2½% semi-annually. Interest charges of 7% annually had to be met.[93] Erlanger and Company eventually paid a $500,000 penalty rather than carry out the terms of the contract. An estimate of the cash realized from the loan would, therefore, approximate $3,000,000 or about one-fifth of the face value.[94] The bonds which remained in the hands of the Confederacy

---

[90] *Ibid.*, Hotze to Benjamin, No. 21, May 9, 1863.

[91] *Ibid.*, Hotze to Benjamin, No. 27, August 27, 1863.

[92] Mason Papers, vol. V, correspondence between Spence and Mason during May, 1863.

[93] See terms of contracts, Mason Papers.

[94] Some of the bonds were cancelled in cotton. It is impossible to estimate accurately the total interest paid on the bonds, or how paid. Some authorities estimate the net cash return from the loan as low as $2,599,000. See Owsley, *King Cotton Diplomacy*, and Schwab, *op. cit.*

were gradually disposed of in one way or another before the end of the war. The misapprehensions of Spence in regard to the loan are at least partially justified, in the light of its complete history.

Funds for the agents remained insufficient. The final payment on the bonds was not made until October, 1863.[95] Much of the cash paid on the first installments was used by Mason to sustain the market. The loan did not release sufficient funds to meet the requirements of the War and Navy Department.

C. J. McRae did not reach Europe until May 13.[96] A few days later Spence and McRae had their first conference. Spence reported that he and McRae agreed on every point.[97] Funds secured from the loan were deposited with Fraser and Company as depositors, this step being required by law. The treasury at Richmond issued treasury warrants against these sums for the various purchasing agents.[98] Spence believed this method of administration would eliminate all discretion in Europe. It would, "narrow General McRae's duties to the signing of the bonds."[99]

More serious than this limitation was the impossible financial situation which the agents faced. They had remained partially inactive for many months awaiting the outcome of the Loan. Orders for supplies and ships were accompanied with letters describing the urgent need in the Confederate States. Secretary Mallory wrote Mason to supply Commander Maury with $5,200,000 out of the Erlanger Loan,[100] a sum greater than the total net cash proceeds from the transaction. Orders for the Ordnance Bureau and Quartermaster's Department could not be filled.

Mallory stated that his department wished to ship cotton to establish exchange which was difficult to provide.[101]

[95] Terms of contract.
[96] Pickett Papers, Hotze to Benjamin, No. 22, May 14, 1863.
[97] Mason Papers, vol. V, Spence to Mason, May 25, 1863.
[98] Ibid., Spence to Mason, June 1, 1863.
[99] Ibid.
[100] Ibid., Mallory to Mason, June 8, 1863.   [101] Ibid.

Others advised the shipment of cotton, or the sale of more cotton certificates. Memminger believed cotton bonds could be sold readily.[102]   Spence was afraid that this would endanger the position of the Erlanger Loan.[103]   Caleb Huse advised the shipment of cotton, having already set an example by loading the Ordnance Bureau steamers with cotton, whenever possible.[104]   He had experienced some difficulty in securing government cotton for vessels.   The average cargo of cotton brought out by one of these vessels had a value of $50,000.[105]   In the summer of 1863, McRae issued a few Naval Store Bonds to meet an emergency in the Navy Department.[106]

Some confusion resulted from the various types of bonds and cotton certificates which had been issued by the Confederacy.   It seems that the first demand for cotton certificates in one form or another, and for the Erlanger Cotton Loan Bonds, was prompted by cotton speculators. The exact nature of these issues were undoubtedly misunderstood by the average speculator.   After several months the various types became better known as investors studied them more critically and tested out their worth in the market.

Uncertainty as to the various types of loans was precipitated in the summer and fall of 1863 when an effort was made to secure the cotton which certain certificates called for.   It developed that the provisions outlined for the redemption of cotton certificates varied.   There were several distinct types.   First of all, there was the cotton certificate which resulted from the Produce Loan in the Confederacy. Cotton accepted by the Confederate officials was stored on plantations or in warehouses at various points.   Certificates were issued against the government cotton which would give the purchaser an absolute right to a particular lot of cotton

[102] Mason Papers, vol. V, June 1, 1863.
[103] Ibid., Spence to Mason, June 1, 1863.
[104] Ibid., vol. VI, Huse to Mason, August 17, 1863.
[105] Ibid.
[106] Ibid., July 25, 1863, Spence mentions these bonds.

with the privilege of shipping the same.[107]   It was this type which Memminger proposed to sell in Europe thinking that it might appeal to some purchasers.[108]   G. N. Sanders carried 1500 of these certificates to Europe in the fall of 1862.[109]

The second type of cotton certificate might more properly be named a cotton bond, as it was alternately called even on the face of the certificate.   An example of this was the Sinclair certificate approved by Mason in an emergency and for a limited amount.   This differed from the treasury certificate in several respects.[110]   It not only called for a specific amount of cotton, but also at a specific price.   Such cotton was to be delivered at any port in possession of the Confederate States Government, within three months after peace between the belligerents in America.[111]   The other Naval Store Bonds were similar to the Sinclair certificates except the price placed on the cotton.

A third type was issued by Caleb Huse and Mason while waiting for the Erlanger proposition to materialize.   It was called a cotton warrant.[112]   They were issued as collateral for the "Merrimac" and its calling for 2,300,000 pounds of cotton.[113]   The warrants issued by Huse to Isaac, Campbell and Company called for cotton at five pence per pound.[114] In the case of Isaac, Campbell and Company temporary and permanent warrants were issued.   For instance, Huse and Mason signed temporary warrants for this firm during January, 1863, representing small allotments of cotton.   These were exchanged within twenty days for permanent warrants representing the cotton in parcels of fifty bales or more.[115]

[107] *Ibid.*, vol. III, Memminger to Mason, October 21, 1862.

[108] *Ibid.*   [109] *Ibid.*

[110] Pickett Papers, Mason to Benjamin, No. 19, November 4, 1862 (enclosure).

[111] *Ibid.*, this might be called the Lindsay Bond as it was designed under their direction.

[112] Mason Papers, IV, 796, 813, February 2, and 5, 1863.

[113] *Ibid.*, also Pickett Papers, Mason to Benjamin, No. 29.

[114] *Ibid.*

[115] *Ibid.*, for examples of temporary and permanent warrants see Mason Papers, III, 599; IV, 730-32, 796-813.

The most conspicuous example of a permanent warrant was signed by Huse on February 2, 1863 for 3,750,000 pounds of cotton.[116]

The Sinclair Certificate and others of its type differed from the Treasury certificates and the Huse warrants in another important essential. In case certificates like the ones used by Sinclair and Maury were not presented for redemption within the specified time[117] they automatically became sterling bonds carrying the usual rate of interest.[118] For this reason they were often called cotton bonds rather than cotton certificates.

In August, 1863, owners of the "Merrimac" certificates asked Huse to sign duplicates in order that the originals could be presented for redemption in the Confederacy.[119] Huse refused, wishing to discourage any attempts to present them before the close of the war. Facilities for getting cotton to the coast were meager and if holders of cotton warrants should call for their cotton, the roads would have to be used for this purpose instead of for Government cotton.[120] Huse already realized the importance of establishing credit abroad by direct shipments of cotton.

Similar attempts were made by certain holders of Erlanger bonds to secure their immediate redemption in cotton. In July, 1863, one investor demanded "to have 16,000 of the loan converted into cotton by delivery of cotton at Charleston within sixty days."[121] The terms of delivery according to the Erlanger contract were " . . . sixty days after such notice the cotton will be delivered: . . . if peace, at the ports of Charleston, Savannah, Mobile, or New Orleans; if war, at points in the interior of the country, within ten miles of a railroad, or stream navigable to the ocean."[122] Mem-

---

[116] *Ibid.*, p. 796, February 2, 1863.
[117] *Ibid.*, usually from one to six months after peace.
[118] *Ibid.*, usually 8%.
[119] *Ibid.*, vol. VI, Huse to Mason, August 17, 1863.
[120] *Ibid.*
[121] Pickett Papers (bound volume), Benjamin to Slidell, July 20, 1863.
[122] *Ibid.*

minger had a legal right to refuse the delivery of cotton at Charleston during the period of the war.

The insistence on the part of the bondholders to exchange them for cotton, and the belief of Slidell that such a procedure would enhance the value of the remaining bonds brought into existence another type of cotton certificate. A contract was made with the Albion Trading Company of London to transport supplies from Bermuda and Nassau to the Confederacy and return to the Islands with cotton.[123] Under terms of the contract, cotton certificates were issued for Erlanger Bonds which in turn were cancelled by cotton brought out by this company.[124] These certificates were sold on the market, fluctuating in price according to the chances of having them cancelled.[125] In October, 1863, McRae informed Secretary of the Treasury Memminger that "Messrs. Erlanger & Co., Messrs. Schroeder & Co., and H. O. Brewer, esq., are about starting a line of small steamers to run from Havana to Mobile in order to bring out cotton under the loan."[126] At this time there were £704,000 of the bonds which had not been disposed of. McRae agreed with Slidell that the credit of the Confederacy at home and abroad could be improved by cancelling the Erlanger bonds as rapidly as possible. Such a procedure would also help provide a market for the bonds on hand.[127] By November, 1864, Slidell had cancelled by cotton or cash, £513,000 of the Erlanger Loan.[128]

Purchases of the agents during 1863 were dependent on the credit received from the Loan and from cotton certificates. The certificates were used only on rare occasions because of the status of the Loan. The end of the year approached with

[123] *Ibid.*, Slidell to Benjamin, No. 52, December 29, 1863.

[124] *Ibid.*, Slidell to Benjamin, No. 59, April 9, 1864; No. 61, May 5, 1864; No. 65, June 30, 1864; No. 71, September 13, 1864; No. 75, November 28, 1864.

[125] *Ibid.*, No. 75, November 28, 1864.

[126] *O. R.*, ser. IV, vol. II, pp. 980-81, McRae to Memminger, October 2, 1863.

[127] *Ibid.*

[128] Pickett Papers, No. 75, Slidell to Benjamin, November 28, 1864.

finances abroad in a precarious position. Isaac, Campbell and Company upon whose credit Huse had made large purchases in 1861 and 1862, accepted a large block of Erlanger Bonds in 1863 in settlement of its account.[129] The Company was forced to dispose of them after a few months at a great loss. McRae expressed his sympathy for this firm on September 15, when he wrote "this house, which has been so much maligned by our overzealous friends, is likely to be ruined by having trusted our Government when nobody else would."[130]

It was not known at this time that the company was keeping two sets of books on Huse's account. McRae spent a great deal of time during 1864 trying to adjust the Isaac, Campbell and Company accounts. Expert accountants were selected to check the books, and it was revealed that there were fraudulent charges in Huse's accounts.[131] McRae offered to arbitrate, and Huse worked industriously to effect a compromise, but a decision was postponed. No satisfactory basis for compromise had been found in October, 1864, the date of the last available dispatch from McRae to the War Department.[132] Huse does not refer to this unpleasant episode in his account of the agents in Europe.[133]

Any attempt to summarize the credit obtained from the Erlanger Loan can be little more than an estimate. The records are not sufficiently complete to enable one to check all of the accounts accurately. In the reports there is some over-lapping, but some general idea may be obtained. It has already been estimated that about $3,000,000 was secured from the £1,500,000 left in the hands of the public after Mason's attempt to sustain the market. From the middle of May until the middle of September, 1863, about £800,000 of the bonds were disposed of.[134] Isaac, Campbell

---

[129] *O. R.*, ser. IV, vol. II, pp. 885-94, McRae to Seddon, October 23, 1863, with enclosures. The bonds amounted to about $1,336,120.

[130] *Ibid.*, enclosure No. 4.

[131] *Ibid.*, III, 528 ff., McRae to Seddon, July 4, 1864.

[132] *Ibid.*; for last dispatches on this question, see pp. 528 ff., 702 ff.

[133] Huse, *op. cit.*   [134] *O. R.*, ser. IV, vol. II, pp. 885-94, 907-10.

and Company took £300,000 of them on which the Confederacy received credit on their account for £267,224 or about $1,335,000.[135] About £500,000 of the bonds bought by Mason were resold during 1863 at various prices, probably averaging 25% discount. After commissions were paid, this probably yielded $1,000,000.[136] This left £704,000 of the bonds on hand on September 15, 1863.[137] In the summer of 1864, McRae secured $750,000 in credit by putting up Erlanger bonds, market price and 25% margin.[138] Only £330,000 of the bonds remained at McRae's disposal. He also sold £98,000 about the same time at very low prices, some as low as 42, in order to meet urgent demands.[139] This yielded some $200,000, and there were £232,000 of the bonds remaining in McRae's hands. If these were disposed of in approximately the same manner as those mentioned in the other transactions of 1864, they would have yielded $575,000. Thus it is not at all impossible that from first to last approximately $6,800,000 was realized from the Erlanger Loan in one form of credit or another.

This amount was obtained at a great sacrifice. The government pledged $15,000,000 worth of cotton at the rate of six pence sterling for each pound of cotton. If we assume that $6,800,000 was obtained from the loan the cotton was actually sold for less than three pence per pound. As a matter of fact, cotton was worth sixty cents per pound in Liverpool during the fall of 1863.[140] Shipping, selling, and such amounted to ten cents per pound. If insurance is figured at 30%,[141] the cotton would be worth thirty-five cents in the Confederacy. It seems, therefore, that the Confederate States through the medium of the Erlanger Loan pledged $45,000,000 worth of cotton to obtain $6,800,000 of credit in Europe for the purchasing agents. On the other

[135] *Ibid.*, p. 887, McRae to Gorgas, August 28, 1863.
[136] *Ibid.*, pp. 885-94, 907-10.
[137] *Ibid.*, p. 908, McRae to Memminger, September 15, 1863.
[138] *Ibid.*, III, 525, McRae to Seddon, July 4, 1864.
[139] *Ibid.*, p. 527, McRae to Seddon, July 4, 1864.
[140] *Ibid.*, II, 985.   [141] Higher than any rate paid.

hand, the bonds proved to be a bad risk for the investor. One-sixth of the total amount was cancelled up to November, 1864,[142] and a very little was cancelled after that. As it turned out, the Confederacy did not actually suffer great loss, but many speculators suffered tremendously.

It should be mentioned that 100,000 bales of American cotton reached Liverpool during the first nine months of 1863,[143] worth on the average, $200 per bale, or $20,000,-000. At this rate, McRae estimated that it would require 260,000 bales of cotton to liquidate the Erlanger Loan.[144] The Confederate Government owned plenty of cotton. Huse demonstrated that Government blockade running was practical. If the Government had shipped cotton during 1863 instead of allowing the profits to go to mercantile companies, her agents in Europe could have shipped abundant supplies to the Confederacy. Private firms such as A. Collie and Company made fortunes out of the business.[145] Memminger has been severely criticized for this apparent neglect.[146]

General Joseph E. Johnston published a book in 1874, premised on the theory that the failure of the Confederate cause was due to the failure of its finances, and placed the blame on Memminger.[147] Johnston stated that the Government should have shipped four or five million bales of cotton to Europe during the first twelve months of the war, an amount which would have formed a basis of credit sufficient for the needs of the Government.[148]

Memminger published an answer to these charges in the "Charleston Courier" in March, 1874.[149] He estimated that it would have taken four thousand ships, allowing one thousand bales per ship, to have carried out Johnston's plan, and that such a fleet could not have been obtained. The

[142] Pickett Papers, Slidell to Benjamin, No. 75, November 28, 1864.
[143] O. R., ser. IV, vol. II, p. 985, McRae to Memminger, October 7, 1863.
[144] Ibid.
[145] Mason Papers, vol. VI, Spence to Mason, December 17, 1863.
[146] Capers, op. cit., pp. 348 ff., especially Joseph E. Johnston.
[147] Ibid.   [148] Ibid., p. 348.   [149] Ibid., pp. 349-50.

cotton could only have been procured by seizure, purchase, or donation. At the first inception of the Confederacy, no one "would have ventured to propose to seize upon the crop then in the hands of the planters, and which furnished their only means of subsistence."[150] And as to purchase, it was many weeks before bonds and notes could be engraved and printed. The demands on the Treasury exceeded the means of supply. "If instead of applying the notes to the daily payments required at the Treasury they had been used to purchase cotton, the Treasury would have found itself filled with cotton, without any money to meet the wants of the government until that cotton could be shipped abroad and sold."[151] The one remaining mode of obtaining cotton according to Memminger would have been donation from the planters. This method was tried especially in the form of a loan, and some 400,000 bales were obtained. "At no time that I am aware of was it in the power of the Government to get possession of the cotton crop, unless it had seized the same by force, and by the same force compelled payment in a depreciated currency; a high-handed course which could never receive the sanction of the statesmen who administered our Government."[152] Memminger also called attention to general expectation that the blockade could not be continued for a year.[153]

Johnston's scheme though far from being possible, might have been carried out on a smaller scale, and probably would have, had not the Confederate Congress and other officials believed that foreign intervention was inevitable.

The South was not disillusioned until the closing months of 1863. These were dark months in the minds of many Southerners and officials of the South in Europe. The Erlanger Loan had proved inadequate to meet the needs of the agents. The bids on Confederate 8% bonds dropped steadily. Cotton certificates could not be used for fear of damaging the future of the loan. Spence wrote to Mason

[150] Ibid., p. 350.
[151] Ibid.
[152] Ibid., p. 351.
[153] Ibid.

in December, 1863, that it was hard to keep his spirits up and he was still of the opinion "that unless we get Europe to move—or some improbable convulsions occur in the North—the end will be a sad one."[154]

But Spence had several reasons for being sad. Just a few weeks before this letter, he had received a dispatch from the Treasury revoking his appointment as financial agent on the ground that McRae and the depositories were sufficient for the duties in Europe.[155] Moreover, he still held £50,000 of the Erlanger Loan which was selling on the market at 37.[156] He had neglected his own business affairs to aid the Confederacy, and his intentions were undoubtedly sincere, but as soon as his hostile attitude toward slavery became sufficiently known, his dismissal was inevitable.[157] Hotze recognized the Government's position, and had, as a matter of fact, kept Benjamin posted on Spence's activities, but he felt that Spence should be compensated for his financial loss. Hotze wrote Benjamin, Spence "contends that while his espousal of our cause arises from sincere conviction . . . he never pretended that he sought a financial connection with the Government without expectation of profit to himself as well as to us . . . and he complained that he is not only disappointed in his just expectation but a loser to a ruinous extent by reason of that connection."[158]

Spence put in a claim for $45,000 to repay his losses,[159] and Memminger authorized McRae to settle for the claim.[160] Memminger and Benjamin wrote Spence polite letters explaining their position, and Mason continued a close friendship with him throughout the war.[161]

Even while acting in the capacity of financial agent, there

[154] Mason Papers, vol. VI, Spence to Mason, December 17, 1863.
[155] Ibid., Spence to Mason, December 7, 1863.
[156] Ibid.
[157] Pickett Papers, Domestic Letters, vol. I, Benjamin to Spence, January 11, 1864; Hotze to Benjamin, No. 31, October 31, 1863.
[158] Ibid., Hotze to Benjamin, No. 31.
[159] Ibid.
[160] Ibid., Domestic Letters, vol. I, Benjamin to Spence, January 11, 1864.
[161] Mason Papers, Mason's Correspondence with Spence.

was very little that Spence could do. The negotiation of Confederate 8% bonds, for which he was first appointed, was never successful. Only a few bonds were sold for they were held off the market because of the low price bid for them, and because of the Erlanger Loan. The cotton certificates and warrants issued by Mason, Huse, and others, served as temporary collateral and were taken up as rapidly as possible.[162] Confederate finance abroad during 1863 was practically limited to the Erlanger Loan. McRae had been appointed agent for the Loan which appointment left Spence little to do except to assist McRae as far as possible.

The funds secured by the various methods just outlined were not sufficient for the purchasing agents, and financial affairs were in a somewhat chaotic condition as the third year of the war drew to a close. Agents in Europe and officials at Richmond gave their thought and energy in a concerted effort to draft a more effective program.

[162] Pickett Papers, Domestic Letters, vol. I, Benjamin to Spence, January 11, 1864; Hotze to Benjamin, No. 31, October 31, 1863.

CHAPTER IV

DEVELOPMENT OF A NEW PLAN

A CONCERTED effort to reorganize the plan of operation abroad was precipitated in 1863 by a number of serious mistakes, abuses, and personal animosities. It is to be remembered that the bitterness between Huse and the two Virginians, Ferguson and Crenshaw, reached its climax in 1863. The reputation of Huse was under a cloud for several months. The same year witnessed the break between Slidell and Spence and the final dismissal of Spence as financial agent. Before the end of the year it was discovered that Isaac, Campbell and Company, from whom Huse had purchased most of his supplies, was practicing fraud in its bookkeeping methods. The Crenshaw-Collie contract was also broken, and Crenshaw and A. Collie severed their commercial relationship. Slidell had become suspicious of De Leon in France and wrote dispatches to the Confederacy designed to undermine De Leon's reputation. Mason and Huse were never on very agreeable terms; they simply tolerated each other. Rivalries and jealousies between navy agents, especially between Lieutenant North and J. D. Bulloch had already developed.[1] There was a conspicuous absence of coördination and centralization of the work being attempted by the various official purchasing agents which was serious enough, but there were other factors which added to the chaotic situation.

Statements from the French Imperial Government and in the Foreign Enlistment Act passed by the British Parliament led officials of the Confederate Government to believe that supplies, including rifles, powder, and unarmed

[1] *O. R. N.*, ser. II, vol. II, pp. 133, 176-77, 204-5, 235-39, 254-56, and *passim*.

ships, could be readily obtained. The various departments of the Government at Richmond were swamped with applications by private speculators for contracts to secure supplies of every kind in Europe. The Government was hard pressed for ready cash, and the Navy and War Departments were desperately in need of foreign supplies. The contractors offered to accept payment in cotton at Confederate ports. Believing such arrangements would speed up shipments, increase the number of blockade violations, and relieve the financial embarrassment of purchasing agents in Europe, the Government made a number of private contracts for supplies.

In every instance an official agent of the Navy or War Department in Europe was appointed to examine the supplies. Few of the private contractors were acquainted with conditions in Europe, and difficulties of all kinds arose. The official agents had to do most of the work, and the private contractors received the benefits. Some of the contracts were impossible of execution; many articles purchased by the contractors had to be rejected because of their inferior quality; there were abundant opportunities to practice fraudulent bookkeeping. Others had little or no money and sought to raise cash in England by selling bonds and cotton certificates in competition with each other and with the official agents. J. D. Bulloch states, "I can say that nothing gave me so much harassing perplexity, or tried my patience and forbearance to so great a degree as the supervision of the private contracts."[2] Bulloch wrote Secretary Mallory on September 24, 1862, describing the outcome of most of these contracts. "A person arrives in England with a contract to build and deliver a ship to the Confederate Government. Being destitute of money himself, his first step is to look up some one who can furnish the necessary capital. Bankers of established position will not engage in such irregular transactions; he is therefore forced to seek for some keen, sharp

_____
[2] Bulloch, *op. cit.*, II, 247.

financier who is ready for any transaction wherein there appears a chance of profit. Such a person being found, the original contractor either sells him the contract outright for a certain named sum, or they agree to divide the profit. The capitalist, not wishing to take the entire risk upon himself, casts about among his friends for aid, each of whom must be assured of a certain gain. . . . To give character to the transaction, all these persons are informed that the ship is for the Confederate Government, and that the Confederate Government is responsible for the payments. The matter is discussed, and soon comes to the ears of those who are dealing directly with the legitimate agents and officers of the Government; the irregularity of the whole transaction is commented upon, and the credit of the Government is measurably injured."[3]

Private contractors reached Europe in increasing numbers during 1863. Mallory, Seddon, Benjamin, Major S. Hart and other noted officials of the Confederate Government appended their signatures to private contracts of one sort or another.[4] They did not understand the conditions abroad, or the confusion which prevailed there until it was too late. Communication with Richmond was slow, and the purchasing agents were somewhat reluctant to point out defects in contracts made by their superior officers.

Major S. Hart at Houston, Texas, with the approval of J. B. Magruder, Major General, commanding the district of Texas, New Mexico, and Arizona, accepted a contract proposed by Mr. Nelson Clements, in December, 1862.[5] Clements agreed to proceed to Europe to procure muskets, rifles, revolvers, shoes, blankets, shirts, hats, and incidentals, the total value of all not to exceed $1,000,000. Clements further agreed to begin to deliver such articles at Matamoras within four months after January 1, 1863, with the under-

---

[3] *Ibid.*, pp. 248-49, Bulloch to Mallory, September 24, 1862.

[4] Mallory, Secretary of Navy; Seddon, Secretary of War; Benjamin, Secretary of State; Hart, Major in War Department and Purchasing Agent to Mexico.

[5] *O. R.*, ser. IV, vol. III, p. 566.

standing that he be paid "on delivery of said invoice 100 per cent. upon invoice cost and charges in cotton on shipboard at the port where said goods are delivered, at 30 cents per pound."[6]

In Europe, Clements made several contracts with Sinclair, Hamilton and Company, which appeared advantageous to every one except the Confederate Government.[7] One of these contracts called for Enfield rifles and other supplies at a cost of £29,813, which according to John Slidell should have been bought for £15,457.[8] Under terms of the contract with the Confederacy, Clements was to receive in advance upon their delivery in Matamoras 100%, which would have netted him 400% on the actual cost price. Payment for the supplies was to be made with cotton at thirty cents per pound although it was actually worth forty-five cents per pound. Thus, he would receive 600% on the invoice price.[9] And this profit, under the terms of the contracts would be had with no risk to Clements, and little to the London firm. The London firm agreed to negotiate for the necessary war risk insurance on the shipment. Clements would not obtain title in the goods until their arrival in Matamoras at which time he would transfer the title to the Confederate Government. S. Hamilton and Company had secured itself by obtaining a promise from Caleb Huse that the Confederacy would purchase the supplies at invoice price if Clements could not meet his obligations at Matamoras.[10] Slidell was of the opinion that Sinclair, Hamilton and Company could not have entered the deal without this promise of Huse.[11]

This contract illustrates several ways by which a private contractor might secure large profits at the expense of the Government. First, Clements was forced to pay a high price

---

[6] *Ibid.*
[7] *O. R. N.*, ser. II, vol. III, pp. 939 ff., May, 1863. It was from this firm that Huse bought supplies to some extent.
[8] *Ibid.*, p. 939, Slidell to Benjamin, October 25, 1863.
[9] *Ibid.*   [10] *Ibid.*, pp. 939-42.
[11] *Ibid.*, p. 939, Slidell to Benjamin, October 25, 1863.

for the supplies, but since his commission was on a percentage basis, this arrangement would redound to his advantage. Second, the invoice was padded. One item in the Hamilton bill was a reported payment by Clements of £1,000 to a Mr. Stringer for having introduced him to Hamilton.[12] This item caused Slidell to note, "it is to the interest of the contractor to pay for everything the highest price and to increase the charges in every way."[13] Third, payment in cotton provided additional remuneration. Fourth, risk for Clements was apparently eliminated and the burden of responsibility was placed on S. Hamilton and Company, and Caleb Huse. Furthermore, Huse had been dealing with Hamilton for more than a year on decidedly better terms than Clements obtained. Clements performed a business transaction similar to those which Huse had been making for many months, the chief difference being that payment was to be made in cotton, but at a price which afforded Clements exceptional speculative reward.

Clements and his associates were finally convicted of outright piracy. In the court-martial trial of Major T. S. Moise, assistant quarter-master of the Department of Texas, considerable evidence was obtained to prove that Moise, Clements, and several others had entered into a fraudulent combination.[14] It seems that under the pretense of procuring supplies for the Government, Moise transferred without authority "the steamer *General Rusk* to his associates without the payment of any price or consideration to the Government; that he authorized them to put her under the British flag by collusive transfer to some British subject, and to employ her in commerce between the Confederacy and the port of Havana for the joint benefit of himself and his associates, without stipulating for any freight or charter money in favor of the Government and without even taking any other security for the return of the vessel to the Government than a

[12] *Ibid.*, p. 933, Slidell to Benjamin, October 9, 1863.
[13] *Ibid.*
[14] *Ibid.*, p. 727, Benjamin to Slidell, March 26, 1863.

bond signed by his associates themselves for the sum of $50,000, which was about one-third the value of the vessel."[15]

The steamer "General Rusk" was carried to Havana, placed under the British flag and provided with British papers, and her name changed to the "Blanche."[16] "After one successful round voyage, in which the parties [involved] made large profits, the *Blanche* was on her way to Havana with a second cargo of cotton when both vessel and cargo were destroyed on the coast of Cuba within the neutral jurisdiction of Spain by the Federal steamer *Montgomery,* under circumstances of such outrage that the Federal Government was forced . . . to make reparation to Spain by the payment of $200,000."[17] One of the parties in Clements' conspiracy went to Europe in an attempt to collect for himself and his colleagues the indemnity paid by the Federal Government to Spain.[18] Benjamin instructed Slidell to "require an explicit assurance that the money shall not be paid to any other party than this Government without its consent."[19]

The Government cancelled the contract with Clements as soon as these facts were known. Thus, the scheme of Clements miscarried, and the plan which promised him untold profit brought him dishonor and financial loss. Some of the supplies which he shipped from Europe eventually fell into the hands of the Confederacy.[20]

A Mr. Chiles of Missouri secured a contract from Colonel Haynes, assistant commissary-general of the trans-Mississippi Department, similar to the Clements' contract. Chiles offered to deliver supplies, shoes, blankets, and cloth, at Matamoras, payment to be made in middling fair cotton at twenty cents per pound delivered at the same port.[21]

[15] *Ibid.*
[16] *Ibid.,* pp. 727 ff.
[18] *Ibid.*
[17] *Ibid.*
[19] *Ibid.,* p. 728.
[20] *O. R.,* ser. IV, vol. III, pp. 565-66, 573; *O. R. N.,* ser. II, vol. III, p. 977. See "Caroline Goodyear" and "Love Bird."
[21] *O. R.,* ser. IV, vol. II, pp. 982-86, McRae to Memminger, October 7, 1863.

Chiles paid an enormous price for the goods as compared with the price paid for similar articles by Caleb Huse. One invoice of Chiles amounted to $1,836,000, but the same articles could have been bought by Huse from Isaac, Campbell and Company for $650,880. Since cotton at this time would net fifty cents per pound in Liverpool, the 9,180,000 pounds which Chiles would receive at twenty cents per pound in payment of his $1,838,000 invoice could have been sold there for $4,590,000. In other words Chiles would receive $4,590,000 for insuring $650,880 worth of goods to Matamoras.[22] None of the goods was contraband, and shipment would be made between the neutral ports of London and Matamoras. Chiles contracted to begin delivery on November 1, 1863,[23] but he asked for an extension of time. Meanwhile, Slidell, Huse, and McRae decided the contract was unfair, and the extension of time was denied.[24] This loop-hole gave them the needed opportunity for annulling the contract.

Secretary Mallory made an arrangement with private contractors for the delivery at sea of six iron-clad vessels, payment to be made in cotton.[25] The contractors had no personal means and they brought pressure on Bulloch to help finance them in England. Some of their papers were captured in a blockade-runner, and the matter was given great publicity. This drew attention to other iron-clad vessels which Bulloch already had under construction. The private contractors were confused with official agents, by the newspapers. This unhappy exposure of a private transaction "contributed to strengthen the complaints and demands of the United States Minister, and served to influence the course adopted by her Majesty's Government in respect to the Liverpool rams, and other vessels alleged to be building for the Confederate States."[26]

[22] *Ibid.*, p. 985.
[23] *O. R. N.*, ser. II, vol. III, p. 932, Slidell to Benjamin, October 9, 1863.
[24] *Ibid.*
[25] Bulloch, *op. cit.*, II, 250-53.   [26] *Ibid.*, p. 252.

These typical cases illustrate the character as well as the impracticability of private contracts. Few, if any, of the contracts ever brought the Confederacy anything except confusion.[27] The apparent reason for resorting to this method of securing supplies was to relieve the financial pressure abroad by using the cotton in Confederate ports. But the multiplication of them in 1863 caused the Confederate officials in Europe to complain. The situation became so acute that Slidell, Mason, Hotze, Spence and others hastened to inform the Government at Richmond that such contracts were disrupting the work of the official agents.

De Leon referred constantly to the confusion which prevailed.[28] At a meeting of Mason, Lamar, McRae, and Slidell, they agreed on the "embarrassment resulting from the employment of numerous agents charged to make purchases and contracts far exceeding the means."[29] A few days later Slidell recommended to Benjamin that the disbursements of the agents of the War and Navy Departments be subject to the control of a common head.[30] Hotze wrote "It is undeniable that the credit of the Government has suffered most seriously by the clashing interests, the rivalries, and hostilities, sometimes the disgraceful public squabbles of contractors, and of the lax manner in which, in many instances contracts appear to have been granted. . . . This great evil is by the many forms of authority . . . the want of precision and vigor. . . . I doubt whether the credit of any other Government of the civilized world would have withstood so successfully and so long as ours has done, such reckless and damaging hauling."[31] He recommended that all private contracts be cancelled for the terms of "these contracts are

---

[27] O. R. N., ser. II, vol. II. p. 644, De Bree to Mallory, April 28, 1864. For other private contracts, see ibid., pp. 644, 670, and passim; O. R., ser. IV, vol. I, pp. 820, 883, 774; III, 1077.

[28] Pickett Papers, De Leon to Secretary of State, No. 6, February 23, 1863; No. 9, August 3, 1863.

[29] Ibid., Slidell to Benjamin, No. 37, June 12, 1863.

[30] Ibid., No. 38, June 21, 1863.

[31] Ibid., Hotze to Benjamin, No. 30, October 3, 1863.

such as to destroy the confidence of prudent merchants, for British commerce however enterprising has no faith in the solvency of a debtor who promises to pay tenfold the value of the goods."[32]

McRae complained of the numerous contractors without capital or credit "hawking their contracts through the London, Manchester, and Liverpool markets and sell them to or divide them with the highest bidder. Such exhibitions are very damaging to our credit, as they create the impression among capitalists and all prudent men that a government which is so reckless of its means is not likely to achieve its independence against such fearful odds."[33]

"To remedy these evils and re-establish the credit of the Government," he suggested the following plan:

First. To revoke or annul all contracts in Europe, in which profits or commissions are allowed, whether they be with agents, contractors, or partners.

Second. That there should be one contracting or purchasing officer each for the War and Navy Departments in Europe. . . .

Third. That there should be one general agent for Europe, who should have the entire control of the credit of the Government abroad, with large discretionary powers. . . .

Fourth. That the government should take the exports and imports into its own hands, and no cotton, tobacco or naval stores should be allowed to leave the country except on Government account or for account of holders of produce bonds. . . .

Fifth. To purchase or take possession of all the cotton and tobacco in the country at a price to be fixed by act of Congress.[34]

Before this dispatch reached the Confederacy the Government had acted on his first three recommendations. The dispatch of Slidell, dated June 12, 1863, recommending a similar plan had spurred the Confederate officials into action. President Davis, Seddon, Benjamin, Memminger, and Mallory planned a centralized agency for supervising finances

[32] *Ibid.*
[33] *O. R.*, ser. IV, vol. II, pp. 983 ff., McRae to Memminger, October 7, 1863.
[34] *Ibid.*; Pickett Papers, Slidell to Benjamin, No. 37, June 12, 1863.

abroad and appointed McRae as head of the department.[35] Seddon wrote McRae "I congratulate myself on having one to whom I can satisfactorily confide the duty of judging and meeting the varying contingencies."[36] McRae was given control over finances, and supervision of orders sent to the different agents.

No choice could have been wiser. No appointment in Europe was more fruitful of results. McRae was a capable business man, with a thorough knowledge of the cotton business, and a man beloved by his associates. The official dispatches of the commissioners and the letters of the various commercial agents and purchasing agents in Europe pay high tribute to his zeal and character. He was the only official of the entire number in Europe about whom no word of disparagement was written.[37] The available records indicate that the friction, jealousy, and confusion which precipitated his appointment was practically eliminated. Thus, the first step toward an intelligent plan for obtaining supplies and for supervising their payment was consummated almost three years after the war started.

The second step, the reorganization of foreign finance based on direct shipments of cotton to Europe, and the related problems of governmental control of blockade running, developed during the next few months.

The same dispatches from Confederate officials in Europe which recommended a centralized agency for European purchases also contained recommendations for raising funds. Before the close of 1863 the use of cotton as a political weapon in Europe was being discredited. James Mason withdrew from England in the fall of 1863.[38] Hope of foreign intervention was not entirely given up this early, but

[35] *O. R.*, ser. IV, vol. II, pp. 824-27, Seddon to McRae, September 26, 1863.
[36] *Ibid.*
[37] Mason Papers; Pickett Papers; Official Records; Trenholm Papers; Willis Collection; Bulloch, *op. cit.*; Huse, *op. cit.*
[38] Pickett Papers, Mason to Benjamin, No. 45 and 46. Mason wrote Russell, September 21, 1863, that he was leaving England.

the situation was decidedly discouraging both in England and in France. But a number of the agents and other officials decided that the use of cotton afforded the most substantial basis for securing funds in Europe. Cotton was worth sixty cents a pound in Liverpool; the government had a supply of cotton on hand with the means of securing more; private commercial houses had grown wealthy in the cotton shipping business; the Ordnance Bureau of the War Department and to some extent the Navy Department had been successful in running the blockade with government ships. What was to prevent the Government from entering the lucrative trade and restoring her credit in Europe? Something had to be done at once. The Erlanger Loan had proven inadequate. Other Confederate bonds were scarcely saleable. Cotton certificates could be negotiated only at ridiculously low prices for cotton. Three years of experience had at least proved what could and what could not be accomplished in the way of foreign finance.

Thus, the same men who had urged the appointment of McRae now urged other drastic measures. They urged the shipment of cotton, and government regulation of the blockade-running. Mason wrote Benjamin, "I would earnestly suggest that arrangements should be perfected, as speedily as possible, by means of fast steamers, for bringing out cotton on Government account."[39] And in regard to the blockade he could "see nothing to prevent the Government taking this whole business into its exclusive hands, and when the cotton is placed at one of the islands, its value is available here at once without further risk."[40] De Leon declared that such a method would be the South's "strongest weapon."[41]

Hotze constantly urged similar measures. He recommended that the Government assume "the strict monopoly of blockade running,"[42] and prohibit the exportation of cot-

[39] *Ibid.*, Mason to Benjamin, No. 43, August 6, 1863.
[40] *Ibid.*, No. 45, September 5, 1863.
[41] *Ibid.*, De Leon to Benjamin, No. 13, December 23, 1863.
[42] *Ibid.*, Hotze to Benjamin, No. 30, October 3, 1863.

ton except for Government account or in redemption of bonds. He thought it expedient to "prohibit the importation of luxuries on any account, and import shoes and clothes as well for the citizens as the army."[43] He also believed that the pecuniary resources if properly marshalled, would enable the South to occupy "a financial position in Europe which would extend recognition sooner than the most powerful arguments of the pen or even of the sword."[44] "If blockade running was constituted an arm of the national defense each would perform only its appropriate work which therefore would be well done. The Treasury would procure without competition the raw materials and regulate the disposition of the proceeds; the Navy—abandoning the hope of breaking the blockade and throwing all its available energies into eluding it—would purchase, build, and man the vessels for this purpose; the agents of the War Department instead of having all these incongruous duties to perform themselves, could give their undivided attention to the important matter of supplies. . . . Our financial transactions will then have acquired such a magnitude that we can command the services of the highest and oldest financial houses, instead of as at present, being left to the mercy of commercial adventurers. . . . It is the only hope of striking the imagination and rousing the action of Europe."[45]

Practically all of these recommendations had been made by McRae in the plan forwarded to Memminger on October 7, 1863.[46] This plan was submitted to the President and his cabinet in January, 1864, and approved. The administration introduced bills into Congress to legalize the measures. The first was entitled, "A bill to impose regulations upon the foreign commerce of the Confederate States to provide for the public defense."[47] It was passed by the Senate on January

[43] *Ibid.*, No. 34, December 26, 1863.
[44] *Ibid.*
[45] *Ibid.*, Hotze to Benjamin, No. 35, January 17, 1864.
[46] *O. R.*, ser. IV, vol. II, pp. 982 ff.
[47] Acts and Resolutions of the Confederate States of America (manuscript in Library of Congress); also "Statutes at Large of the Confederate States,"

19, by the House, January 23, and signed by Jefferson Davis, February 6, 1864.[48] The most important provision specified that the exportation of cotton, tobacco, military and naval stores, sugar and rice from the Confederate States was forbidden except as the President should regulate.[49] An act "to prohibit the importation of luxuries or of articles not necessaries or of common use,"[50] was signed by Davis on the same date. The act prohibited the importation of strong drinks, furs, rugs, laces, toys, fireworks, furniture, velvets, jewelry, paintings, and similar articles.[51]

The policy adopted by the President toward blockade running was summarized in the following regulations:

First. That every vessel owned by private persons shall be considered on every voyage as chartered to the Confederate Government for one-half of her tonnage, outward and inward.

Second. That all private owners of cargo exported from the Confederacy shall bring in return supplies equal to one-half the proceeds of their expected cargo.

Third. That the several States shall remain at liberty to charter the other half of each vessel, and shall be free to carry out or bring back cargo on that half without being subject to the regulations.[52]

It should be noted that for several months previous to the above act, the War Department had required all vessels "to devote one-third of their tonnage to the use of the Government."[53]

An agreement was made by the Treasury, Navy, and War Departments on April 14, and approved by Davis on April 18, for the purchase and transportation abroad of tobacco, cotton, and naval stores.[54] An appropriation of $20,-

1861-1864 (Richmond, 1864), chap. xxiv, p. 81. See also O. R., ser. V, vol. III, pp. 78-80, 80-82.
[48] Ibid.
[49] Ibid. (adapted).
[50] Ibid.; see "Statutes at Large," chap. xxiii, p. 79.
[51] Ibid.
[52] O. R., ser. IV, vol. III, p. 554.
[53] Ibid., p. 954.
[54] O. R. N., ser. II, vol. III, pp. 897-99, Benjamin to Memminger, Seddon and Mallory, Sept. 15, 1863; O. R., ser. IV, vol. II, pp. 824-27, Seddon to McRae, Sept. 26, 1863.

ooo,ooo was made by Congress for the purchase of such stores, and Thomas L. Bayne, Lieutenant-Colonel, was appointed to supervise the enterprise.[55] Bayne was already acting as representative of the War Department in the management of Government steamers purchased by the Ordnance Bureau, and of steamers under various partnership contracts.[56] This was the beginning of a plan corresponding with the reorganization under McRae in Europe, for centralized control of cotton at home.

But it was a long and tedious process with numerous difficulties to be overcome. The acts passed by Congress aroused a storm of protest from several sources. First of all the commercial houses attempted to induce a relaxation of the regulations, and to bring pressure on the Government by allowing their vessels to remain idle. But after several weeks of negotiations trade was resumed and the number of vessels actually increased.[57] "Among the efforts made to induce a change of the regulations, was a warning . . . [that] they would transfer their vessels to the Executives of the several States and thus withdraw them from the operations of the regulations."[58]

The fifth section of the Act of February 6, to regulate foreign commerce provided, "That nothing in this act shall be construed to prohibit the Confederate States, or any of them, from exporting any of the articles herein enumerated on their own account."[59] State owned vessels were not subject to regulations, but state chartered vessels were. The Confederate Government maintained that the provisions applied to all vessels except those owned outright by the several states.[60] This provision prevented the owners of vessels from chartering them to state governors, with whom they

[55] O. R., ser. IV, vol. III, p. 370, Bayne to Seddon, May 2, 1864.
[56] O. R., ser. IV, vol. II, p. 660 (Special Orders, No. 174).
[57] Ibid., III, 554, Davis to House of Representatives, June 10, 1864.
[58] Ibid.
[59] Confederate States of America (Ms.); also O. R., ser. IV, vol. III, p. 953, Trenholm to Davis, December 12, 1864.
[60] Ibid., pp. 950 ff., Davis to House of Representatives, December 20, 1864.

could make better bargains than with the Confederate Government. The governors of several of the states objected to the new policy and attempts were made to amend or repeal the act.[61]

Obviously the regulations left one-half of each vessel open for charter by the State, and Jefferson Davis insisted that this was sufficient.[62] George A. Trenholm, now Secretary of the Treasury agreed with Davis.[63] The owners of the vessels shared the opposition with the governor. It was argued that if a state should acquire the use of one-fourth of a steamer the Confederacy should relinquish an equal portion. But Trenholm and Davis refused to concede this point.[64] The states and the blockade running interests were never able to alter the regulations, although agitation never ceased.

It will be remembered that several bureaus and departments of the Government and of the states had been purchasing small amounts of cotton for many months prior to 1864. Two questions were immediately presented when the reorganization of purchases under Thomas L. Bayne was inaugurated. Should the various departments continue the supervision of the purchase of cotton, and what disposal should be made of the cotton already owned by the departments? As to the last question, a regulation was passed which provided for the transfer to the Treasury Department of the cotton owned by the various departments.[65] This was not accomplished without some difficulty,[66] the most serious obstacle being the contracts payable in cotton made by the various departments.[67] This policy of making payments in cotton at a Confederate port for supplies contracted for by the several bureaus was discontinued as soon as possible,[68]

---

[61] *Ibid.*, pp. 897, 950 ff.   [62] *Ibid.*, p. 950.
[63] *O. R.*, ser. IV, vol. III, pp. 953-55, Trenholm to Davis, December 12, 1864.
[64] *Ibid.*, pp. 948-54.
[65] See Laws and Regulations of Act of February 6; also *O. R.*, ser. IV, vol. III, p. 371, Bayne to Seddon, May 2, 1864.
[66] *Ibid.*, pp. 364-65, 423-24, 781-85, 899-901, and *passim.*
[67] *Ibid.*   [68] *Ibid.*

for the contracts usually called for cotton at less than one-half of its actual value. The policy might have been discontinued earlier if the Confederacy had not been limited in transportation facilities.[69]

As to the question of the continuance of individual cotton purchases by each bureau or department, Colonel Bayne said it "would entail upon the agents of the War Department the very complications it has been so long the object to get rid of. Every bureau and department would have a cotton account, and it would be difficult, if not impossible, to bring forward to the ports the proportion needed by the several bureaus and departments."[70] He favored the plan of having "at each port one stock of cotton and one disbursing agent, who would pay for such importations and freights as were chargeable to any department of the Government."[71] This plan was perfected by the summer of 1864, and all the funds made available to the depositories at Liverpool were made subject to the control of General McRae for the supply of the purchasing agents of the several departments.[72] Estimates were made of the needs of the departments, and warrants were issued by the Treasury upon the depositories, under which the funds would be available to General McRae as fast as cotton could be shipped.[73]

Bayne's responsibilities were increased as the plan was perfected. He was charged with the "purchase, repairing, compressing, and shipment of cotton, . . . with the purchase and receipt of foreign supplies, to be paid for in cotton; and, incidentally, with most of the foreign correspondence of the War Department."[74] This necessitated some oversight of the available ports and inlets for shipping purposes, and internal transportation.[75] In October, 1864, he made ap-

[69] *Ibid.*, especially pp. 423-24, Bayne to Seddon, May 13, 1864.
[70] *Ibid.*, p. 370, Bayne to Seddon, May 2, 1864.
[71] *Ibid.*
[72] *Ibid.*, pp. 587-89, 955; also *ibid.*, II, 550-51, 416, 968-82, 525-30, 587-90, 1071-73, for purchases under the old system.
[73] *Ibid.*, III, p. 588, Trenholm to Seddon, August 12, 1864.
[74] *Ibid.*, pp. 1071-73, Bayne to Breckinridge, February 9, 1865.
[75] *Ibid.*

plication for an additional £15,000,000 to finance the under-
taking.[76]

The new plan was welcomed by the commissioners and
the agents in Europe. Slidell was pleased, and he wrote
Benjamin that the hope of influencing European powers to
deny the obligatory force of the blockade by practical illustrations of its efficiency was blasted; that blockade running
for individual account had become an "almost unmitigated
nuisance."[77] He was glad that the Government had taken
the business under its control. Hotze was pleased with the
prospects of the new plan.[78] He had appealed to the political sagacity, to the justice, and to the humanity of Europe in
vain. He was happy to make Europe pay its share of the
cost of the war in the increased cost of cotton.[79]

The legislation and regulations were in accord with Mc-
Rae's wishes. He wrote Seddon, "I hope the Government
will not allow the outside pressure to cause any future modification of these regulations, and, above all, that for a mo-
mentary necessity you will not allow the agents at the islands
to make contracts with steamers granting privileges not in
accordance with these regulations."[80] He suggested that the
Government purchase the remaining interest in all partnership contracts or annul them.[81] The Ordnance Bureau had
a large partnership contract with the Mercantile Trading
Company,[82] and there were many other contracts, notably
those with Crenshaw, and with the Albion Trading Company. The Albion Trading Company objected strenuously
to the regulations imposed by the Confederacy in April,
1864.[83] This Company, it may be remembered, was en-

---

[76] *Ibid.*, p. 778, Bayne to Seddon, October 10, 1864. See also pp. 1071-73,
Bayne to Breckinridge, February 9, 1865.

[77] Pickett Papers, Slidell to Benjamin, No. 49, April 9, 1864.

[78] *Ibid.*, Hotze to Benjamin, No. 48, August 6, 1864.

[79] *Ibid.*, No. 35, had anticipated this action.

[80] *O. R.*, ser. IV, vol. III, pp. 525-30, McRae to Seddon, July 4, 1864.

[81] *Ibid.*, p. 528.

[82] Alias C. H. Reid and Company.

[83] *O. R. N.*, ser. II, vol. III, pp. 1244-46, Slidell to Benjamin, November
28, 1864.

gaged in bringing out cotton with which to cancel cotton bonds. Slidell interceded in its behalf, because he considered the contract highly advantageous to the Government.[84] He apparently did not realize that the Government would receive more from a half ship load of cotton on Government account, than on several ship loads to cancel bonds which called for cotton at six pence per pound. McRae planned to annul all similar agreements as soon as he could purchase and build ships to take care of the business.[85]

In anticipation of the new plan, and after he learned of its development, McRae launched a comprehensive program for securing ships to run on Government account. The judicious management and industry of McRae created favorable comment in Europe, and the Erlanger Loan rose ten per cent within a few weeks after his official appointment.[86] It continued to rise as his shipping projects under the new system began to materialize.

McRae made an arrangement with a well known firm, J. K. Gilliat and Company to establish a line of steamers to run on Government account. He borrowed money on Erlanger Bonds to start the enterprise.[87] Fraser, Trenholm and Company financed him in a program to secure eight first class steamers to be purchased or built under the direction of J. D. Bulloch.[88] McRae and Bulloch negotiated for fourteen steamers, the last of which would be delivered in the spring of 1865.[89]

In order that the needs of the various departments might not suffer until the fleet of blockade runners was ready, McRae made a contract with Alexander Collie and Company of London to ship supplies for a period of six months.[90] This contract was not especially favorable but was signed as an

---

[84] *Ibid.*
[85] *O. R.*, ser. IV, vol. III, pp. 525-30, McRae to Seddon, July 4, 1864.
[86] Pickett Papers, Hotze to Benjamin, No. 35, January 17, 1864.
[87] *O. R.*, ser. IV, vol. III, p. 525, McRae to Seddon, July 4, 1864.
[88] *Ibid.*; Bulloch, *op. cit.*, II, 237 ff.
[89] *Ibid.*
[90] *O. R.*, ser. IV, vol. III, pp. 529-30, for copy of contract.

emergency measure. A. Collie and Company agreed "to provide four large and powerful new steamers" to carry out quartermaster, ordnance and medical stores.[91]

The Government already owned four steamers which had been in the service of the Ordnance Bureau, in addition to three-fourths interest in five steamers operated by Crenshaw. Under McRae's program, therefore, twenty-seven steamers would be placed at the disposal of the Government as rapidly as they could be purchased or built. It has already been noted that six of the steamers bought or built under McRae's arrangements reached the coast in time to make one or more trips through the blockade before the close of the war.[92] It is probable that the system would have been in full swing by the summer of 1865 if military defeat had been postponed. But the chief ports of Wilmington, Savannah, and Charleston, favorite landing places for Government vessels because of railway connections to Richmond and other central points, were taken by the North early in 1865. After February, 1865, blockade running was most profitable to ports in the Gulf of Mexico.[93] Galveston and other Texas cities thrived for a brief period as ports for blockade runners.[94] Some cotton was exported from the shallow inlets and rivers along the coast, and modest amounts of supplies run in.[95] Only those vessels of which the draft of water did not exceed six feet were practical for this purpose.[96]

Though the war ended before the maximum benefits could accrue from the new plan which was perfected in 1864, a great deal was accomplished. A measure of credit is due McRae for the part which he played in perfecting the new system. Several of its features came as the result of his

[91] *Ibid.*
[92] Bulloch, *op. cit.*, II, 243.
[93] Owsley, *King Cotton Diplomacy*, pp. 279 ff.
[94] *Ibid.*; also William Watson, *The Adventures of a Blockade-Runner*, pp. 286-87; Willis Collection.
[95] *O. R. N.*, ser. II, vol. II, p. 804, Mallory to Moffitt, Feb. 24, 1865.
[96] *Ibid.*

sagacious advice. Even more credit is due him because he was able to put it into operation at his end of the line without any criticism. The agents in Europe gave him their hearty coöperation, which enabled him to complete his plans rapidly and without friction. The plan was one of the most intelligent bits of strategy ever formulated by the Confederacy. That it appealed to the commercial world is attested by a series of events which followed its initiation.

McRae wrote Seddon on July 4, 1864, that the credit of the Confederacy was rapidly improving, and "by proper management will soon be available for all our wants."[97] He stated, "by the end of the year the Government will have the means in its own hands to obtain all the supplies required abroad. . . ."[98] The Erlanger Loan rose from 42 in the spring of 1864 to 77 in August.[99] Hotze enthusiastically wrote, "The new commercial system, though scarcely yet in its infancy, has thus far worked so beneficially as to promise when fully developed to fulfill literally and even to exceed my own glowing anticipations."[100] He expressed the opinion that no amount of pressure upon the Government should induce it to depart from "the policy which dictated these salutary measures."[101]

But considerable pressure was brought to bear upon the Confederate Congress to modify its policy. Jefferson Davis wrote Seddon and Trenholm for a statement of the result of the plan as they had observed it. Seddon answered the inquiry on December 10, 1864.[102] He believed that the legislation had been highly beneficial and that the individual states had not been discriminated against in the regulations. For a time commercial houses sought to embarrass the Government by discontinuing the use of their blockade runners, but Seddon notes that "The number of vessels engaged in running the blockade has steadily increased since the estab-

[97] *O. R.*, ser. IV, vol. III, pp. 525-29, McRae to Seddon, July 4, 1864.
[98] *Ibid.*
[99] Pickett Papers, Hotze to Benjamin, No. 48, August 6, 1864.
[100] *Ibid.*   [101] *Ibid.*
[102] *O. R.*, ser. IV, vol. III, pp. 928-30.

lishment of the regulations and is now larger than ever before. Many new steamers are understood to be on the way to engage in the business."[103] Furthermore, "the regulations have been beneficial to the Confederate States Government in furnishing the means abroad to purchase supplies and munitions of war and the tonnage required to transport them to our ports."[104] He concluded, "It would be exceedingly inexpedient to repeal the act, and experience has not suggested to me any modification or amendment as necessary."[105]

Trenholm concurred that the regulations had been beneficial and should not be modified. He pointed to the fact that blockade running was still highly profitable for the owners under the new regulations. Shares in all blockade stocks commanded an enormous price in the market.

President Davis in his message to the Senate on December 17, and to the House on the 20th summarized his attitude toward the legislation in question.[106] He reminded Congress that the legislation was passed to remedy evils in the commercial system. It was the consensus of public opinion prior to the laws of February 6, 1864, that the foreign commerce of the Confederate States "was almost exclusively in the hands of aliens; that our cotton, tobacco, and naval stores were being drained from the States, and that we were receiving in return cargoes of liquors, wines, and articles of luxury; that the imported goods, being held in a few hands and in limited quantities, were sold at prices so exorbitant that the blockade-runners, after purchasing fresh cargoes of cotton, still retained large sums of Confederate money, which they invested in gold for exportation and in foreign exchange, and that the whole course of the trade had a direct tendency to impoverish our country, demoralize our people, depreciate our currency, and enfeeble our defense."[107] Davis

---

[103] *Ibid.*
[104] *Ibid.*   [105] *Ibid.*
[106] *Ibid.*, pp. 948-53, with enclosures.
[107] *Ibid.*

stated that every one recognized that a remedy was desirable and stated, "My conviction is decided that the effect of the legislation has been salutary; that the evils existing prior to its adoption have been materially diminished, and that the repeal of the legislation or any modification impairing its efficiency would be calamitous."[108] This opinion he stated "is shared by every Executive Department that has been intrusted with the execution of these laws and regulations, and thus enabled to form a judgment based on observation and experience."[109]

His arguments were enforced with facts. He cited instances to prove that blockade running was still profitable for commercial firms. "The shares of one company, originally of $1,000 each, were selling in July last for $20,000 each, and now command $30,000. Those of another company have increased in the same period from $2,500 to $6,000; and all exhibit a large advance."[110] The plan, continued Davis, had "put an end to a wasteful and ruinous contract system. . . . Instead of being compelled to give contractors a large profit on the cost of their supplies, and to make payment in cotton in our ports at 6 pence per pound, we now purchase supplies abroad by our agents at cost in the foreign market, and pay there in cotton, which sells at a net price of 24 pence per pound."[111] According to estimates made by Davis, 100 bales of cotton exported by the Government would purchase the same amount that 600 bales would under the private contract system.[112]

The reports of T. L. Bayne on the shipment of cotton under the new system include some interesting facts. On July 1, 1864, the purchase and shipment of cotton by the individual bureaus and departments was abandoned, and all cotton was shipped to the account of the Treasury Department. Most of the cotton was shipped to the islands in small blockade runners which carried on the average about two

[108] Ibid.
[109] Ibid.
[110] Ibid.
[111] Ibid.
[112] Ibid.

hundred bales of cotton for Government account.[113]   For instance the "Ella" carried 191 bales, the "Lynx" 268 bales, the "Annie," 190 bales, the "Lucy" 152 bales.[114]   A few runners carried as much as 700 bales, and several carried as little as 25 bales.   Of 10,412 bales of cotton shipped by Bayne before November 1, 1864, only 1037 bales were captured, leaving a net of 9,375 bales.[115]   In other words, approximately one-tenth of the cotton shipped failed to reach the Sea Islands, a remarkable showing for a period in which the blockade was supposed to be very effective.

Of the 10,412 bales shipped during the above mentioned period, practically all of it was sent to Nassau.   In fact, 8,101 bales were shipped to Nassau, 164 to Halifax, 1,954 to Bermuda, and 193 bales to Havana,[116] most of them from Wilmington and Charleston.   Of the total amount, 5,602 bales were shipped from Wilmington, 4,534 bales from Charleston, 75 bales from Mobile, 83 bales from Savannah, 68 bales from St. Marks, Florida, and 50 bales from Bay Port, Florida.[117]   The loss of Wilmington and Charleston early in 1865 was a severe blow to the export of cotton.   But the shipments continued through December.   Approximately 1,300 bales were shipped during November and something over 4,000 bales in December is explained in part by the arrival of new blockade runners arranged for by McRae.

In his report as of December 10, Seddon stated that 27,299 bales of cotton had been shipped under the new plan.[118]   This would net according to his estimate $5,296,-006 equal in Confederate currency at 25 to 1, $132,400,-150.[119]

Meanwhile, the importation of supplies indicated the revived credit at the disposal of the purchasing agents.   With the year ending November 1, 1864, the reports show that Bayne received for the cis-Mississippi Department 136,832

---

[113] Trenholm Papers, portfolio I.
[114] Ibid.
[115] Ibid.
[116] Ibid.
[117] Ibid.
[118] O. R., ser. IV, vol. III, p. 930.
[119] Ibid.

small arms, 1,490,000 pounds of lead, 1,850,000 pounds of saltpeter, and 6,200,000 pounds of meat, besides miscellaneous supplies of all kinds.[120] From October 31 to December 4, twenty-six blockade runners attempted to run in with Confederate supplies to Wilmington alone. Of the twenty-six vessels, twenty-three were successful; one was captured, one destroyed, and one was beached.[121]

One can only guess at the possible results of the new system had it been inaugurated earlier. Hotze's English publication, the *Index*, stated, " 'Had the cotton been exported for its own account, instead of, for the most part, private speculators, the Confederate Government might have dispensed with foreign loans, might have bought its warlike stores at the lowest cash rates and supplied its citizens with commodities of prime necessity at a moderate advance on cost.' "[122]

It is probable that many Confederate officials had realized the possibilities in such a system for many months. The suggestion that the Government enter the business of blockade running and control her exports was suggested to Benjamin in January, 1862.[123] But the Confederacy was playing for higher stakes. She believed that foreign intervention, or repudiation of the blockade could be hastened by the policy which she vainly pursued. It was logical that such intervention would come. After waiting three years without making any progress, she resorted to the expedient of capitalizing on the economic value of her chief staple.

Bankers and financial executives in Europe were evidently impressed by the new financial system adopted by the Confederacy. They believed that sufficient credit could be secured in Europe to pay for war supplies and to revive the depleted financial condition in the Confederacy. Con-

---

[120] *O. R.*, ser. IV, vol. III, pp. 953-55, Trenholm's report to Davis, December 12, 1864.

[121] *Ibid.*, pp. 955-58, Baynes' report from October 25 to December 6, 1864.

[122] Owsley, *King Cotton Diplomacy*, p. 416, quoted from Index.

[123] *O. R.*, ser. IV, vol. I, p. 829, R. Salas to Benjamin, January 2, 1862.

sequently secret negotiations began in June, 1864, to carry out this idea.[124]

An agent of a group of European bankers wrote Memminger on June 11, 1864, that they wished to establish a Confederate bank in Europe with a capital of £10,000,-000.[125] They wished to obtain charters from one or more southern states which would enable them to establish branches at the different cities in the South. Such a plan would facilitate bringing out new loans in Europe, and they would advance a considerable sum in cash to prove their good faith. After the war the capital would be used to encourage trade and to develop the resources of the South. Citizens of the Confederacy would be allowed to subscribe one-third of the stock before or after the war at par value.[126]

No more is heard of the plan until December, 1864, when Trenholm received a letter from B. S. Baruc, dated December 9, 1864, outlining the plan in detail.[127] Baruc, as agent for Mr le Comte Berle' de Chauvigny and associate bankers, stated the terms upon which negotiations might be brought to a successful issue. The contract contained five pages with twenty articles, but the chief items were as follows:[128] First. The European financiers offer to negotiate a loan for the Confederate States for fifteen million pounds sterling, at seven per cent, and amortisable within twenty-five years. Second. If and when the preliminary contract is signed Chauvigny will place £500,000 to the credit of the Confederacy in any French bank designated by the Confederate authorities. Third. The Confederate Government will have an Act passed by Congress which will legalize the contract, and will use its good will to obtain from the state of South Carolina the charter for a branch bank. Fourth. One-half of the net proceeds of the loan will be placed to the credit of the Confederate Government; the other half of the proceeds are to be applied exclusively for the purchase of

---

[124] Trenholm Papers, for full story of these negotiations.
[125] Ibid.   [127] Ibid.
[126] Ibid.   [128] Ibid. (adapted).

Confederate paper currency in circulation, both in the shape of bonds and Treasury notes. Fifth. The security for this loan shall be a fixed amount of cotton of which the Government now holds a portion, and the rest shall be raised by taxation or otherwise. Sixth. The contractors shall be entitled to certain fees and commissions, one per cent on the loan, two per cent for all expenditures, obtaining of good will, and other such considerations.

Trenholm answered Baruc's letter on December 13, by replying that, "the terms are quite acceptable and I will negotiate at once for power to carry out the contract."[129] He also promised to use his influence in securing the charter for the bank from the legislature of South Carolina.[130] Two days later Trenholm wrote Davis for authority to execute the loan.[131] He stated, "nothing would contribute more to restore the value of the currency or to relieve the pressure upon our finances generally than such a loan, and I strongly recommend the proposals to your favorable consideration and action."[132]

Meanwhile, a bill was presented to the Legislature of South Carolina to obtain a charter for the said bank. The "Act to establish the Franco-Carolina Bank" passed both houses on December 23, 1864.[133] It provided for a bank with fifty-two and one-half million francs capital stock, to be located in Charleston or some other town in South Carolina. The state of South Carolina pledged to subscribe one-twentieth of the stock.

The negotiations were carried on with the utmost secrecy. James Mason was chosen to represent the Confederacy in Europe until the loan could be placed on the market. This selection of Mason was made because of the family connec-

---

[129] *Ibid.*, Trenholm to Baruc, December 13, 1864.
[130] *Ibid.*
[131] *Ibid.*, Trenholm, to Davis, December 15, 1864.
[132] *Ibid.*, Trenholm to Davis, December 17, 1864.
[133] *Ibid.*, telegram from W. L. Trenholm to G. A. Trenholm. A copy of the act may be found in the Trenholm Papers.

tion of Slidell with Erlanger. Slidell's daughter had married Erlanger's son.[134]

The secret act to "issue a further foreign loan" was rushed through Congress early in January, 1865, and approved by Davis, January 4.[135] It authorized the Secretary of the Treasury and the President to negotiate a loan not exceeding £15,000,000 sterling.

Duncan F. Kenner was appointed to proceed to London and Paris on behalf of the Treasury Department to complete the negotiations.[136] It was understood that the charter for the South Carolina bank would not be used if the loan was not negotiated. Trenholm warned Kenner to avoid one of the mistakes made in the case of the Erlanger Loan, that was, to bring out the loan at a fairly low price. The Erlanger Loan was offered at 90; Trenholm believed that this loan should not be offered above 70.[137]

The military disasters which the Confederacy suffered immediately after these negotiations put an end to the enterprise. But the fact that European bankers considered this plan practicable seems to indicate that financial circles had faith in King Cotton and in the new financial system of the Confederacy.

[134] *Ibid.*

[135] *Ibid.*

[136] Kenner, a member of Congress from Louisiana, was selected to carry instructions to Mason and Slidell to approach the French and English governments on the question of recognition in return for emancipation. This phase of Kenner's Mission is well known. See, J. H. Latané, *A History of American Foreign Policy;* Owsley, *King Cotton Diplomacy.* But, it is not generally known that Kenner had a double mission.

[137] *Ibid.*

CHAPTER V

MEXICO AS A PORT OF ENTRY AND SOURCE OF SUPPLIES

THOUGH the Confederacy concentrated her efforts of diplomacy and commercial relations in England and France, her southern neighbor was by no means neglected. It was considered extremely desirable, if not absolutely necessary, to maintain friendly relations with Mexico. Mexico has been made a sort of international football on several occasions, and one of these instances was during the period of the American Conflict. As a neutral nation bordering the Confederacy, immense possibilities for trade were apparent. Moreover, the success of Slidell and Mason in Europe might depend on the turn of politics in Mexico.[1] This episode includes primarily the work of the Confederate representatives dispatched to strategic points in Mexico, and the trade relations which Mexico carried on with individuals and officials of the trans-Mississippi Department.

The hope of encouraging a friendly commerce with Mexico was not the only item which prompted the Confederacy to send her diplomats to that turbulent country. As the only neutral nation bordering the Confederacy, friendly relations might mean the difference between victory and defeat. Eminent dangers would result from any other relationship. Protection from irresponsible raiding bands of Mexicans and renegades along the Texas border was paramount. Moreover, the strong unionist element in West Texas, by joining forces with a number of Texans who wished to have a national flag of their own, could jeopardize the position of the Confederacy in that territory.[2]

The traditional policy of the South had been one of ex-

[1] Owsley, *King Cotton Diplomacy*, chap. iv for diplomatic phases.
[2] *Ibid.*, p. 88.

pansion, and Mexico was naturally suspicious of the Confederacy. Open alliance could hardly be expected, but recognition of the Confederacy and a break with the North might precipitate such an alliance. It was a prize worth working for. "The friendship, the commerce, the recognition, and the active alliance of Mexico were extremely important."[3]

Relations with Mexico were complicated by the unstable condition of her Government. For several years preceding the war between the states, Mexico had been suffering from internal dissensions, and revolution.[4] There were two rival factions, the so-called Liberal party and the Church party. From 1855 to 1861 several presidents were elected and then set aside in rapid order. The Church party as representative of wealth and privilege was discredited, and Santa Anna, the dictator, had fled. Benito Juarez, supported by several liberal states in the western and northern parts of Mexico, was selected to lead their faction and installed at Vera Cruz as president on June 1, 1858.[5] The reactionary party with General Zuloaga as president set up its government in Mexico City early in 1858.[6] War between the two factions continued unabated until 1861.

Then there were several powerful states especially in the northern part of Mexico which were not party conscious. Santiago Vidaurri led one powerful group of states.[7] For several years Vidaurri was the undisputed governor of Nuevo Leon and Coahuila. His influence was considerable in the surrounding states of Tamaulipas, Sonora, and Chihuahua. He dreamed of an independent government, under his leadership, bordering the Río Grande. This ambition prompted him to cater to each of the conflicting parties and to render aid to the weaker party in order to preserve the balance of power and to destroy any centralizing tend-

[3] Ibid.
[4] H. T. Priestley, The Mexican Nation, pp. 317 ff.
[5] Ibid., p. 332.
[6] Ibid., pp. 321-29.   [7] Ibid., pp. 332 ff.

ency.[8] Juarez was successful in ousting the government at Mexico City, and the struggle temporarily subsided in January, 1861.[9]

Four months later John T. Pickett, on the nomination of John Forsyth, was appointed special agent of the Confederacy to Mexico City.[10] Before the war, Pickett, as United States consul at Vera Cruz, had openly favored the annexation of Mexico. Now he was given the opportunity to prosecute his theory by advocating a union between Mexico and the Confederate States.[11] Robert Toombs outlined certain arguments which might be used by Pickett in Mexico. Intimate relations would be helpful to both countries in the securing of cheap goods and low freight rates. A friendly Confederacy could protect Mexico from foreign invasions. Toombs argued that both nations were agricultural, and that their needs and interests were mutual.[12] Pickett was authorized to seek recognition if a favorable opportunity was presented, but above all to negotiate a treaty which would assure favorable commercial possibilities.[13] It was further suggested that Pickett encourage privateering, and obtain if possible, the permission to use Mexican ports for Confederate battle ships and for prizes taken on the high seas.[14]

Agents of the United States, especially Thomas Corwin, proved to be able rivals in the diplomatic game. Toombs anticipated this in his instructions, "It will be your duty to use all the means at your disposal to watch the proceedings of the representative of the United States at Mexico and prevent the Mexican Government from taking any step at his suggestion which would be prejudicial to the interests of the Confederate States, and give them just cause for interrupting those relations of friendship and good neighborhood which it is the earnest desire of this Government to preserve

[8] *Ibid.*, pp. 335-36; Owsley, *King Cotton Diplomacy*, p. 92.
[9] Priestley, *op. cit.*, pp. 336-38.   [10] Pickett Papers, I, 9612, 9627 ff.
[11] *Ibid.*, pp. 9627 ff. for instructions and pp. 9636 ff. for other instructions and suggestions given by R. Toombs.
[12] *Ibid.*
[13] *Ibid.*   [14] *Ibid.*

and improve. . . . Remind them [the Mexicans] that Southern statesmen and diplomatists . . . have always been the fast friends of Mexico."[15] Pickett's record as an expansionist and his hearty contempt for the Mexicans did not prevent his accepting the instructions with bravado. He wished to do even more. He suggested that it should be his duty to purchase munitions, to discourage possible border raids, and to use a million dollars if necessary to obtain information and good will.[16]

In Vera Cruz, Pickett renewed the friendships of his consular days. Among his acquaintances was Senor Mata, a close friend of Juarez, and a member of the Mexican Congress. A lengthy and cordial correspondence ensued,[17] both men were masters in the art of duplicity; they were tricksters of the same hue. Pickett tried his art on Governor Don Ignacéo de la Llave of Vera Cruz, who assured Pickett of his friendship and promised to maintain a policy of neutrality.[18]

Pickett moved on to Mexico City after a brief stay in Vera Cruz. He discovered that public opinion in the capital was favorable to the North. Agents of the United States had probably been energetic in spreading anti-southern propaganda. At any rate, Pickett ceased to be a diplomat. By losing his temper, he further alienated citizens and officials in the Juarez Government. When questioned as to his mission in Mexico, he replied that his primary duty was "to recognize Mexico—provided I can find a government that will stand still long enough."[19] On hearing the rumor that the United States had obtained permission to pass troops over a section of Mexico into Arizona, he informed his associates that the Confederacy would immediately dispatch thirty thousand diplomats across the border into Mexico.[20]

The Juarez government learned of these and other similar remarks. His indiscreet phrases were valuable material

---

[15] *Ibid.;* also *O. R. N.,* ser. II, vol. III, pp. 202-8.
[16] Pickett Papers, I, 9636 ff.   [17] *Ibid.,* June, 1861.
[18] *Ibid.,* Pickett to Toombs, June 27, 1861.
[19] *Ibid.,* Pickett to Toombs, July 11, 1861.
[20] *Ibid.*

in the hands of Corwin. Pickett courted both the Liberal and the Church parties, but constantly lost ground. The influence of Corwin was tremendous, and Mexico continued suspicious of Southern aggression. Pickett's correspondence, intended for the authorities in Richmond, in which he reviled the Mexican character and disclosed his motives in Mexico, were intercepted. He became involved in quarrels and was thrown in jail for criminal assault.[21] After thirty days behind the bars he succeeded in escaping. His usefulness was completely destroyed, and he returned to the Confederacy to join the army.[22]

The most important agent ever dispatched to Mexico by the Confederacy was Juan A. Quintero.[23] He was a Cuban by birth, a citizen of Texas, and a loyal patriot of the South. Having resided in Mexico for many years, he was particularly fitted for this mission. He was first sent on a temporary mission to Monterey, "to assure the governor that the wish of this government is to maintain the most cordial intercourse with the people of Mexico, to prevent border raids, disorders and lawless invasions of the soil of Mexico by our citizens, but we require that this friendly disposition be reciprocated."[24]

Quintero immediately won the coöperation and possibly the confidence of Vidaurri. At Vidaurri's request he was appointed as permanent agent of the Confederacy at Monterey. Vidaurri agreed to use his powerful influence in checking the border disturbances, and to work out reciprocal trade agreements. He became, in fact, an active ally of the Confederacy.[25] He was willing to go farther in the way of open alliance than President Davis thought expedient.[26] However, the friendship proved invaluable for the South.

[21] *Ibid.*, No. 13 and No. 17.

[22] *Ibid.*, II, 9714 ff.

[23] *Ibid.*, Quintero's correspondence; J. Fred Rippy, *The United States and Mexico*, pp. 234 ff.

[24] *Ibid.*, Toombs to Quintero, May 22, 1862.

[25] *Ibid.*

[26] *Ibid.*, Browne to Quintero, September 3, 1861; *O. R. N.*, ser. II, vol. III, pp. 253-55.

It became Quintero's responsibility to direct the trade between Mexico and the Confederacy, to supervise the trade with Europe which came through Mexico, to deal with the delicate question of border disturbances, and to keep on good terms with the Juarez Government, the Church Party, and the resourceful Vidaurri.

Early in 1862, Vidaurri obtained nominal control of the state of Tamaulipas. This opened the important seaport, Matamoras, to the Confederacy.[27] It was to this port that a considerable amount of European goods destined for the trans-Mississippi Department were shipped. In August, 1862, Quintero was able to report favorably on the Mexican trade. "Texas," he wrote, "is well supplied with ammunition," secured through the states controlled by Vidaurri.[28] Almost every necessary article could be obtained in Mexico except small arms. The trade between Texas and the states of New Leon and Coahuila expanded rapidly.[29] Hundreds of teamsters and wagons were engaged in the "freight" business. It was reported that powder, lead, copper, tin, blankets, coffee, sugar, hides, chalk, and cloth could be secured in abundance.[30] Quintero wrote that he could put five hundred wagons to hauling cotton out of Texas to sell or exchange for supplies.[31]

As the opportunity to trade and speculate in cotton increased, traders flocked to Matamoras and other trade centers near the border. Ships were anchored at the available harbors seeking Texas cotton, the trade unit most desired by the importers. The problem of obtaining cotton and transporting it across long stretches of semi-arid and desert regions of West Texas and Mexico became acute. The government was harassed by conflicting interests and competition among the cotton agents of the various states, bureaus, and

[27] Pickett Papers, Quintero to Browne, March 22, 1862.
[28] Ibid., Quintero to Benjamin, August 14, 1862.
[29] Ibid., September 24, 1862.
[30] Ibid.
[31] Ibid., October 19, 1862.

departments. It was the same old story of decentralized control, with its inevitable consequences.

The vast territory adjacent to Mexico, commonly known as the trans-Mississippi Department, was associated most intimately with Mexican commercial relations. It is only in the light of the complicated history of this Department and of its bureaus that the confusion which resulted from the cotton trade can be understood.

This territory was at first divided into several departments, and then given a semblance of unity by designating it as the trans-Mississippi district of the Western Department.[32] A few months later, in May, 1862, it was broken into two districts and called the trans-Mississippi Department.[33] The Texas district included Texas, and a portion of western Louisiana. The Arkansas district included Missouri, a part of northern Louisiana, and the state of Arkansas.[34] In July, 1862, General Holmes was placed in command of the department. He immediately reorganized the territory into three districts. The whole of Louisiana was set aside as one district, the Indian territory was added to Arkansas, and New Mexico and Arizona added to the Texas district.[35]

Inefficiency in administration and fear that the Department would be severed from the other parties of the Confederacy through the loss of the Mississippi River, prompted the unification of the Department by President Davis. General E. Kirby Smith was placed in command on March 7, 1863. He administered the Department through Major General Magruder in Texas, Major General Holmes in Arkansas, and Major General Taylor in the Louisiana district. A complete government was set up with the various bureaus and departments as maintained at Richmond. Shreveport, Louisiana was ultimately selected as the seat of government.[36]

[32] O. R., ser. I, vol. III, p. 826, January 12, 1862.

[33] Ibid., IX, 713, May 26, 1862.

[34] Ibid., LIII, 819.   [35] Ibid., IX, 791, August 20, 1862.

[36] For additional details concerning organization and history of the trans-Mississippi Department, see O. R. (especially ser. I, vol. VII, p. 826; IX,

From Shreveport, General Smith ruled over an expansive territory. Much of it was thinly populated and void of railroads. Transportation and communication to the furthermost sections were slow and tedious. Yet, it is this territory which profited most by the trade across the Rio Grande. Extensive trade was first inaugurated between Matamoras and Brownsville, and between Monterey and San Antonio.[37] Brownsville continued as an important trade and military post until its capture by the Federals in November, 1863. In the absence of railroads and direct water routes, much of the cotton and articles of trade had to be hauled in wagons. A route was opened up from Brownsville to East Texas by way of the famous King Ranch, to Alleyton. There was probably a short stretch of railroad between Roma and Alleyton.[38] Another favorite route was from Monterey to Laredo or Eagle Pass by San Antonio and thence to various points in central and West Texas. Still a third route ran from Rio Grande city to Laredo and Gonzales.[39]

Wagon trains journeyed long distances, part of which had little grass, or water. A drouth in 1862 added to the wretchedness of the parched and windy plains. There was constant danger along the border from brigands; teams were scarce, and teamsters could hardly be found; and, above all the government found that cotton was difficult to obtain. This trouble was caused in part by the influx of cotton speculators, and by competition between the various agents of the government with each other and with private contractors. Major Simeon Hart was dispatched by the War Department

---

713 ff.; XXI, 279 ff.; XXII, 772 ff.; LIII, 804 ff.); Charles W. Ramsdell, "The Texas Military Boards, 1862-1865," *Southwestern Historical Quarterly*, XXVII, 253-76; Florence E. Holladay, "The Powers of the Commander of the Confederate Trans-Mississippi Department," *Southwestern Historical Quarterly*, XXI, 279-98, 333-59; Rippy, *op. cit.*; Trenholm Papers.

[37] Pickett Papers, Quintero to Benjamin, August 30, 1862.

[38] *Ibid.*, Quintero to Browne, November 6, 1861.

[39] *Ibid.*; also Ramsdell, *op. cit.*, p. 263.

to purchase cotton in Texas and exchange it for supplies.[40]
He was a well known frontiersman and had friendly contacts
with leading business men at Monterey and Matamoras. A
corps of assistants were placed under his supervision. The
state of Texas placed its agents in the field in competition
with Hart. Hamilton P. Bee, in charge of the provisional
army at Brownsville, bought and sold in the open market according to his official needs. General Magruder of the
Texas district was forced to resort to a similar policy in order
to obtain supplies. Competition caused a rapid appreciation
in cotton values. The situation was chaotic.

To remedy the evil, Kirby Smith established a Cotton
Bureau, under the control of Colonel W. A. Broadwell.[41] A
branch office of minor importance was set up at Monticello,
Arkansas.[42] The most important sub-bureau was set up at
Houston, Texas, and was known as the "Texas Cotton Of-
fice."[43] First, A. W. Terrell, and within a few weeks,
Colonel W. J. Hutchins, was placed in charge of the Texas
Bureau.[44] Hutchins was given the military rank of Lieu-
tenant-Colonel, and a military order was issued to serve as
a charter.

The Cotton Bureau was a compromise between the military and the farming interests, the object being to procure
cotton by voluntary act of the planter, rather than by impressment.[45] Prior to its establishment, the chaotic and
competitive buying, with its consequent evils had induced the
military authorities to prohibit the exportation of cotton except under certain restrictions. Impressment was threatened
and in some cases enforced against persons attempting to
violate the instructions. Successful pretexts were often devised for evading the regulations. Private contractors posed

[40] O. R., ser. I, vol. XV, p. 866; ibid., LIII, 882-83, Hart to Myers, June
8, 1863.
[41] Ibid., XXII (pt. ii), 835, August 3, 1863.
[42] Trenholm Papers, portfolio I.
[43] O. R., ser. I, vol. XXVI (pt. ii), pp. 535-39.
[44] Ibid.; also Trenholm Papers, full report of work of "Texas Cotton
Office."   [45] Ibid.

as Government agents, and the people were unable to discriminate between official and private agents.[46] The operations of the Government were characterized as dishonest, and farmers withdrew their support.

In the meantime, supplies arrived at the Rio Grande, and the Government found itself embarrassed for lack of cotton with which to make payment. An order was issued to seize 20% of all cotton arriving on the Rio Grande. This policy created distrust and dissatisfaction among the holders of cotton, and the uncertainty had a tendency to limit the introduction of supplies. The needs of the army were pressing, and after much discussion the Cotton Bureau was established as an experiment.[47]

Hutchins was well known as a capable business executive, and his assistants were chosen from outstanding Texas merchants. The order issued by Kirby Smith and which served as the Bureau's charter stated that it should obtain by sale or agreement, all cotton that the Government might require for the purchase of army stores of all kinds; all Government officers, agents and contractors, engaged in the purchase or removal of cotton in or through Texas were placed under its jurisdiction; applications for all contracts based on cotton or for exemptions from impressment must go to Hutchins; cotton in transit was made subject to impressment if necessary to relieve the immediate necessities of the Department; existing liabilities of the Government were assumed by the Bureau's acting under absolute authority and being liable only to Colonel Broadwell.[48]

The general plan upon which the bureau proceeded was further outlined: full publication of the plan should be made for the benefit of the public; the cotton growing sections should be broken into districts with a capable business man appointed thereto to represent the bureau; central depots

---

[46] *Ibid.*, report of Hutchins.
[47] *Ibid.*
[48] *Ibid.*, Special Orders, No. 198; see *Senate Document*, ser. 987, 62nd Congress, 3rd session.

should be established at Alleyton, Brenham, Halletsville, Lagrange, San Antonio, and other strategic points, with a trusted purchasing agent in charge; transportation facilities were to be centralized when possible; the service of conscripts should be obtained through the bureau of conscription; all reports were to be made to the seat of Government.[49]

Hutchins immediately published the plan for the benefit of an anxious public.[50] He reviewed the chaotic condition which prevailed and the extreme need of the Department. His plan was to purchase one-half of the cotton of the planter, or holder, and upon its delivery at a Government depot give exemption against military impressment for a like quantity. For the cotton sold to the bureau, cotton certificates were given for its specie value to be paid for in cotton bonds or such other equivalent as congress should provide. Transportation facilities of the district were encouraged by allowing liberal freight rates payable in cotton. Hutchins promised that impressment would be resorted to only after the failure of other methods.[51]

Finally, an appeal was made to the good sense and the patriotism of cotton holders. "The plans of this office are well matured, its policy will be permanent, its course consistent, impartial and firm. If proper confidence and assistance are extended to us by you, we feel confident of the best results toward thoroughly equipping our armies for our defense, restoring and increasing Government credit, checking unlawful speculation, appreciating the value of cotton in the hands of the people, enabling them to procure their needed supplies. We appeal to you, shall there not be united, harmonious, active, efficient coöperation, by devoting a portion of your cotton to the great duties of the crisis, the successful defense of Texas from enslavement and devastation?"[52]

---

[49] *Ibid.* (adapted from the memorandum added to Special Orders above cited)
[50] Trenholm Papers.
[51] *Ibid.*   [52] *Ibid.*

The plan was generally approved. The price of cotton on plantations rose in a few weeks from three to six cents per pound. Large contracts were made for baled and unbaled cotton. The baled cotton near railroads came in rapidly, but the scarcity of bagging and rope prevented an immediate accumulation for delivery of the bulk of the cotton.[53] Measures were taken to provide this material, and the supply of cotton for supplies appeared secure.

Unfortunately for the plan, Pendleton Murrah, the Texas governor, interposed a State Plan for the acquisition of cotton to be exported for State purposes.[54] His negotiations involved the purchase of 40,000 bales of cotton, and the chief items in the plan of the bureau were adopted. The Governor's Military Board, which was under his control, took over the cotton business under the State Plan. In the resultant competitive buying between the State and the Confederate agents, the Confederate agents were at a distinct disadvantage. State agents actually helped their friends evade the Confederate officials.[55] State agents bid up the cotton rapidly to fifty cents per pound, whereas the agents of the bureau could offer only fifteen and sixteen cents per pound.[56] The State made payment in specie interest bearing bonds which offered such superior attractions to the people, above the certificates of indebtedness issued by the Cotton Office, that the Confederate States soon lost control of most of the cotton previously contracted for.[57] Texas offered superior advantages to contractors, thereby securing a practical monopoly on transportation facilities.[58] Governor Murrah further blocked the Confederate agents by sponsoring sentiment against impressment, and by having anti-impressment laws passed by the Texas legislature.[59]

[53] *Ibid.*
[54] *Ibid.;* also Ramsdell, *op. cit.*, pp. 269-70; O. R., ser. I, vol. XXIV, pt. ii, pp. 1103-6; LIII, 971-75, 958-59, 1016.
[55] *Ibid.*, XXIV (pt. ii), 1103-4.
[56] *Ibid.*, LIII, 971-75; Trenholm Papers, portfolio I.
[57] Trenholm Papers, portfolio I.   [58] *Ibid.*
[59] O. R., ser. I, vol. LIII, p. 1016, Trenholm to Seddon, July 21, 1864.

General J. B. Magruder of the Texas District added to the troubles of the bureau in attempting to supplement its work by providing supplies for his army through cotton shipments.[60] Hutchins constantly urged legislation which would place the bureau on an authoritative basis. The need for a law to provide a method of liquidating the cotton certificates was especially pressing.

In June, 1864, Kirby Smith invoked the use of large discretionary power in order to secure cotton and supplies. He issued an appeal to the citizens of the trans-Mississippi Department to coöperate. Munitions, clothing and medicine were necessary. "It is left to you" he stated, "whether for the preservation of your homes you will force the government to resort to impressment."[61] On the same date he issued authority to bonded officers to obtain one-half the cotton in the Department, by impressment if necessary, for the purchase of naval and military stores.[62] Hutchins was placed in charge of the purchase of supplies.

Three days later he issued orders for the regulation of all overland trade to Mexico.[63] These regulations were similar to those issued by the Confederate Treasury and War Departments on February 6, 1864.[64] Smith proposed to use military force if necessary to insure compliance with the regulations. It was provided that all stores intended for exportation into Mexico be registered with the collector of customs, and a permit issued for them; exportations should be on account of the Confederate States or of some individual state; a rigid control of importations was provided for; Major A. H. Willie was dispatched to San Antonio to supervise the regulations.[65]

The regulations were in harmony with the new plan

[60] *Ibid.*, pp. 955-59; XXXIV, 822 ff.
[61] Trenholm Papers, June 1, 1864.
[62] *Ibid.*, General Orders, No. 34, June 1, 1864.
[63] *Ibid.*, General Orders, No. 35, June 4, 1864; also *O. R.*, ser. I, vol. XXXIV, pt. iv, pp. 643-44.
[64] *Ibid.*, ser. IV, vol. III, pp. 206-7.
[65] Trenholm Papers, General Orders, No. 35.

adopted by the Confederacy in February, 1864, to control exports and imports. Hutchins did not favor the use of impressment. He recommended a plan to place the cotton certificates on a competitive basis with Texas bonds. Conditions did not materially improve under Smith's regulations.

In August, 1864, the purchase and shipment of cotton were centralized under the Treasury Department, and the Cotton Bureau abolished. P. W. Gray was appointed Treasury agent for the trans-Mississippi Department. His duties corresponded with those of Thomas L. Bayne, who was so successful in the territory east of the Mississippi.[66] Broadwell was assigned to the Commissary Department, and Hutchins was made assistant secretary for the same.

Thus, the Cotton Bureau which was established as a compromise between the military and the planter came to an end. Military connection with the cotton trade and the purchase of supplies was discontinued. The Cotton Bureau was attacked by a storm of criticism and opposition from the beginning. It was never sufficiently legalized, and the opposition led by the State of Texas, private contractors, and military leaders prevented an effective program. Yet, its labors were not all in vain. To label it as a failure would be to overlook many important accomplishments.

The bureau provided emergency funds and credit during a critical period. It sustained the credit of the Government at a time of destitution in the army. At the beginning of the war, most of the arms and the munitions in Texas were in possession of the United States troops. The available arms were issued to the soldiers first organized and carried to Arkansas, Missouri, and to the cis-Mississippi region. Few arms were ever imported into the trans-Mississippi region from the east.[67]

The first efforts of Hutchins and his associates were to procure arms and ammunition to the neglect of clothing and other stores. With some apprehension, Hutchins accepted

---

[66] O. R., ser. I, vol. LIII, pp. 1016-18; XLI (pt. iv), 1133.
[67] Trenholm Papers.

the position as chief of the Texas Office, but he was converted to the program of the bureau. In November, 1864, he wrote, "Many of the guns and most of the powder which gained the victories at Mansfield and Pleasant Hill and won the campaigns in Louisiana and Arkansas were procured by the Cotton Office. . . . The force with which Colonel Benevides kept the enemy on the Rio Grande in check, the expedition under Colonel Ford which retook Brownsville and the present force which now holds the Rio Grande, have been mainly supplied and supported through the instrumentality of the Cotton Office and Cotton Bureau. . . . For twelve months past the entire supply of the army in this Department with articles from abroad has been through this agency, and many supplies purchased previously to the organization of the Texas Cotton Office have been paid for, almost totally without expenditure of money by the Government. . . ."[68]

Available records indicate that over 72,000 bales of cotton were purchased by the bureau.[69] Whether the Government actually obtained control of this amount is doubtful. Hutchins reported that only 15,000 bales were actually acquired by the Texas Cotton Office during the six months of its existence and that Broadwell obtained 17,000 bales from other sources during the same period.[70] But there is some justification for the belief that the army was more adequately supplied during the months immediately following the reorganization of the Department by Kirby Smith in June, 1864.[71] If this is true, evidently Smith was more successful than the old Cotton Bureau in obtaining cotton. Cotton was not obtained in sufficient quantities to liquidate the debts made by the bureau.[72]

[68] Ibid.
[69] United States Senate Document, ser. 987, 62nd Congress, 3rd session, pp. 262-307.
[70] Ibid.
[71] Ibid. Hutchins stated in November, 1864, ". . . Most gratifying results have followed, . . . a large amount of supplies have been obtained. The army is better supplied than ever previously."
[72] Ibid.

The centralization of authority under the Treasury Department promised to eliminate the chief evils with which the Cotton Bureau had to contend. Imports and exports were carefully controlled under the new plan. Supply depots were established on the islands near the coast and at Matamoras. Mexico removed the trade restrictions on the cotton trade, and general conditions along the border appeared to be much improved by 1865.[73] The military disasters which came thick and fast in 1865 changed the whole picture.

While Smith, Broadwell, Hutchins, and other officials of the trans-Mississippi were making every effort to regulate and systematize the cotton business at home, Quintero and Fitzpatrick were busily engaged with the acute problems in Mexico.

Richard Fitzpatrick was appointed Commercial Agent to Matamoras in November, 1862.[74] Insufficient authority, lack of ready communication, and ill health prevented his rendering any conspicuous service. The duty of maintaining friendly relations and of keeping open the channels of commerce in and through Mexico fell largely to Quintero and to the Confederate generals in command of the western subdistrict of Texas. Benjamin watched Mexico and Texas with suspicious eyes. Early in the war, he wrote Slidell that France might help Texas withdraw from the Confederacy. She had at least two very good reasons for making such a move; first, to establish a buffer state between Mexico and the Confederacy; and second, to provide for an independent source of cotton supply.[75] The most serious problems relating to commercial relations between Mexico and the Confederacy were internal rather than international, economic rather than political. Trade relations between the Confederacy and Europe were inseparably associated with dip-

[73] Pickett Papers, Quintero to Benjamin, November 5, 1864.
[74] Pickett Papers, *Domestic Letters,* vol. I, Benjamin to Fitzpatrick, November 15, 1862.
[75] *Ibid.,* Benjamin to Slidell, October 17, 1862.

lomatic relationships. However, the economic and the political were not completely divorced.

The trade with Mexico continued throughout the war with only an occasional interruption. The most important single factor in the maintenance of cordial relations with the border states was Quintero. He received some valuable advice from Richmond and some admirable coöperation from Kirby Smith, Magruder, Bee, Slaughter, and McCulloch. The most significant factor from the Mexican side was Governor Vidaurri. Fortunately Quintero and Vidaurri remained on working terms most of the time. President Juarez was favorable to the United States, but he was too busy with his own affairs to injure seriously the Confederate cause.

Border raids and filibustering proved to be among the most serious and delicate problems with which Quintero and his associates had to deal. There were a number of bandit chieftains notably, Cortinas, Carvajal and Zapata, who gave no end of trouble. Posing as patriots of Juarez, they were able to maintain a considerable following. In sympathy with Juarez they delighted in annoying the Confederacy by attacking the commerce and by stirring up strife and bitterness along the border. Renegade Texans furnished some of the brains and the man power for various exploits from Texas into Mexico, and from Mexico across the border into the Confederacy.

Carvajal, in spite of his long record as a bandit, and enemy of Vidaurri, counted a number of influential Texans among his friends. In 1862, he established headquarters in Brownsville, Texas, and recruited Mexicans and nondescripts for raids into Mexico.[76] Vidaurri very justly complained to Quintero for the lack of reciprocity on the part of those whom he had befriended. Quintero realized immediately the seriousness of the situation. Juarez wished to close the Mexican border to the Confederacy, and Vidaurri was the

[76] Rippy, *op. cit.*, pp. 89 ff.

only man who could do it successfully. After protesting without success to the Governor of Texas and to Colonel Ford at Brownsville, Quintero appealed to Benjamin for prompt action. Quintero explained that Colonel Ford had actually given friendly aid to Carvajal, and that friendly relations with the Governor of the border states were fast dying out. He believed that the good will of Vidaurri was essential to the welfare of the Confederacy and that retaliatory measures would certainly be instituted by him unless Carvajal could be deterred from his marauding escapades. Quintero concluded his letter to Benjamin, "I consequently request the Department to appoint a person to succeed me, who may have more influence than myself with the military of Brownsville and avoid the serious difficulties I believe to be near at hand."[77]

Vidaurri retaliated by levying import, transportation and harbor duties of various kinds, and a duty of two cents a pound on cotton exports. Quintero shrewdly pointed out to Vidaurri that such a measure would harm himself as well as the Confederacy. A large portion of his income was the customs received along the border from the Confederate trade. Vidaurri consequently repealed some of the duties.[78] In the meantime, Ford had been ordered to arrest Carvajal and to put an end to his raids. Pressure was then brought to bear on Vidaurri by Quintero to repeal all export duties on Mexican goods shipped into the Confederacy. In this he was temporarily successful.[79] But Quintero waged a constant fight to keep the various duties down. He had trouble with the Juarez Government on the same point. Juarez failed to obtain the eleven million dollars from the United States, and he constantly levied duties of one sort or another to replenish his impoverished treasury.[80]

[77] Pickett Papers, Quintero to Benjamin, March 28, 1862; also Quintero to Browne, March 22, 1862, and to Benjamin, July 5, 1862.
[78] Ibid., Quintero to Browne, April 17, 1862.
[79] Ibid., Quintero to Benjamin, July 5, 1862.
[80] Ibid., Quintero to Benjamin, August 30, September 24, October 12, and November 21, 1862.

With Carvajal out of the way, Quintero breathed a sigh of relief, but his troubles were just beginning. The administration in Tamaulipas changed hands about this time, and General Traconis, the new Governor, allowed Zapata and certain renegade Confederates to use his state as a base of operation for raids into the Confederacy. Encouraged by the United States consul, and under the United States flag, a motley band under Zapata made a terrific onslaught along the Texas border.[81] Wagon trains were attacked, the teamsters murdered, and the property confiscated or destroyed. The Confederacy retaliated by seizing at Matamoras several leaders of the troublesome group and disposing of them.[82] The Governor of Tamaulipas demanded the return of the prisoners and urged Juarez to close the Mexican border as a retaliatory measure. General Bee, in command at Brownsville, negotiated for the safe return of all the prisoners except one or two who had been buried in the soil of Texas.[83]

The United States consuls played a conspicuous part in sponsoring similar atrocities.[84] It is unnecessary to mention all of them, but border trouble continued, with brief intervals throughout the war. Quintero had other vexing situations to untangle besides the border raids. As an outstanding example of a commercial mix-up was the seizure of Confederate funds by a relative of Vidaurri, Patricio Milmo. Milmo and Company was an outstanding commercial firm at Matamoras. It speculated heavily in cotton, and furnished more supplies to the Confederate agents than they were able to pay for. Milmo and Company played a rôle in Mexico similar to the one played by Isaac, Campbell and Company in England. Purchases and payments were complicated by the competition and conflicting orders of Confederate agents.

Major Hart, agent for the War Department, at Matamoras, made large contracts for army supplies. He had

---

[81] *Ibid.*, Quintero to Benjamin, January 30 and February 26, 1863.
[82] *Ibid.*, March 21, 1863.
[83] Owsley, *King Cotton Diplomacy*, p. 133.
[84] *Ibid.;* also Quintero makes constant mention of the part taken in the raids by United States officials.

been authorized to purchase cotton with which to liquidate his debts.[85] This he found almost impossible because of the interference of agents appointed by Magruder. State agents and private contractors further complicated the cotton business.[86] Hart could not obtain cotton to pay his debts. Major Russell, Quartermaster appointed by Magruder, seized shipments of cotton intended for Hart and applied the proceeds on debts incurred by his own department. He also purchased cotton for the Cotton Bureau. Cotton came to the border slowly in 1863, partly on account of a drouth in West Texas and limited transportation facilities.

Milmo and Company had played for handsome rewards. Not only had the firm advanced Major Hart abundant supplies on his promise to pay, but it had financed others engaged in the cotton trade.[87] Patricio Milmo, the son-in-law of Vidaurri, commanded tremendous political power, which made him a dominant influence in the commercial relationship with Confederate agents. But its methods changed when it became impossible for Hart to pay his bills promptly. Milmo became associated with unscrupulous contractors, and took a militant attitude toward Confederate agents. An attempt was made to obtain fabulous prices, and damage suits of various kinds were brought against the Confederacy. A number of unfair contracts had been made with various firms associated with Milmo and Company.[88] Hart refused to abide by some of the contracts. The lack of harmony between Hart and Russell added to the confusion.

One contract especially, precipitated a heated controversy. Hart ratified a contract with Milmo for the delivery of a million pounds of flour. It was stipulated that

[85] *Ibid.*, Fitzpatrick to Benjamin, July 15, and October 22, 1863.

[86] *Ibid.*, Quintero to Benjamin, January 30, 1863.

[87] For a full story of Milmo and Company as well as other similar stories see, *ibid.*, Quintero's dispatches during 1863-1864; also *O. R.*, ser. I, vol. LIII, pp. 930-51.

[88] Pickett Papers, Quintero to Benjamin, September 11, 1863; February 9, 1862, Quintero to Hunter, November 10, 1861.

100 pounds of flour would be exchanged for 85 pounds of cotton. By December, 1863, most of the flour had been delivered, but Hart did not have sufficient cotton to pay for it. Hart paid the remainder in Confederate currency at a great loss to Milmo.[89] Milmo became exceedingly anxious about the account when Brownsville was captured by General Banks.[90] He therefore seized other Confederate property to make up for the loss.

C. C. Thayer, agent for the Confederate Treasury Department, arrived in Matamoras, November 6, 1863, with fifteen million dollars in Confederate money for the trans-Mississippi Department. The unscrupulous Cortinas was in power at Matamoras at the time Brownsville had been captured, and the uncertainty of the general situation caused Thayer to seek a method of safe conveyance for the funds.[91] Russell suggested that the funds be placed in the hands of Milmo who could transport them by way of Monterey to Eagle Pass, and in the Confederacy. Because of Vidaurri's friendship and the relation of Milmo to him as son-in-law, Thayer was pleased with the suggestion. He was glad to turn the dangerous job over to such a powerful and reliable firm. Having made the necessary arrangements, he journeyed to Monterey to await the shipment.[92]

Milmo then notified Hart and wrote Thayer that the funds would be held until the Confederate debts were paid.[93] Quintero protested to Vidaurri that such an act was a breach of international law.[94] Vidaurri, who was probably interested in the financial success of Milmo and Company, refused to act. He suggested that Quintero take the matter

[89] *Ibid.*, Quintero to Benjamin, December 23, 1863.

[90] *Ibid.*, Quintero to Benjamin, November 9, 1863. It was believed in official circles that the burning and evacuation of Brownsville was perpetrated to cover up wholesale stealing by Major Russell and business firms. (*Ibid.*, Fitzpatrick to Benjamin, March 8, 1864).

[91] *Ibid.*, Fitzpatrick to Benjamin, November 17, 1863.

[92] *Ibid.*, Quintero to Benjamin, December 23, 1863.

[93] *Ibid.*

[94] *Ibid.*, also Pickett Papers, Quintero to Benjamin, January 25, 1864.

to court. This Quintero quite properly refused to do because the courts were controlled by Vidaurri.[95]

Quintero then appealed to Benjamin and suggested that retaliatory measures be taken. He wrote of the uncertainty of Vidaurri's friendship, "He promises Juarez today, what he promised yesterday to the Regency, and what he will promise tomorrow to Doblado and Gonzales Ortega."[96] Quintero and Hart appealed to Kirby Smith, who immediately ordered an embargo on cotton and prohibited the departure of Mexican property from Texas.[97] Vidaurri soon came to terms. The funds were released and the Confederacy made arrangements to pay its debts with Milmo and associated companies.[98] It was discovered that Major Russell, who had given Hart so much trouble, had been bribed by Milmo and Company. Consequently he was given a dishonorable discharge by the President.[99]

In the spring of 1864, President Juarez was forced by the Imperialists to retreat eastward. Governor Vidaurri fled, and Juarez entered Monterey early in April. In spite of grave danger to his own life and misgivings in regard to trade possibilities with the Juarez Government, Quintero stood his ground and sought an interview with Juarez. Juarez received him cordially, invited him to dinner, and introduced him to his cabinet.[100] Moreover, he convinced Quintero that he expected to keep the channels of trade open to the Confederacy.[101] Patricio Milmo was arrested as a partner of Vidaurri, and his property confiscated. Vidaurri's secretary of state crossed the Rio Grande into Texas but was seized by General Hamilton, U. S. A., returned to Matamoras, and shot by Juarez. In return for this good deed,

---

[95] *O. R.*, ser. I, vol. LIII, pp. 930-51 reviews the chief incidents in the story.

[96] Pickett Papers, Quintero to Benjamin, January 25, 1864.

[97] *Ibid.*, February 1, 1864.   [98] *Ibid.*, February 28, 1864.

[99] *Ibid.*, Fitzpatrick to Benjamin, March 8, 1864; *O. R.*, ser. I, vol. XXXIV, pt. II, pp. 1030-33; LIII, 930-51.

[100] Pickett Papers, Quintero to Benjamin, April 3, 1864.

[101] *Ibid.*

General Hamilton and General Heron ordered Juarez to arrest Quintero and other Confederate agents. Juarez assured Quintero that he expected to maintain a neutral policy and that political offenders against the Federals would not be molested.[102]

During the few months that Juarez remained in the territory formerly controlled by Vidaurri, trade relations were exceptionally cordial and prosperous. Quintero remained the key man for the Confederacy. His diplomatic tact, his thorough understanding of the Mexican character, and his business ability can hardly be disputed.

In the fall of 1864, the French and imperial forces swept every power before them, and Juarez fled for his life.[103] Vidaurri had a few months before found refuge and honor with the French. In October, 1864, the French took possession of Monterey and Matamoras. Quintero proved equal to the exigencies of the situation. He reported that the Confederate position remained favorable.[104] In the last dispatch which reached Benjamin, Quintero was optimistic. The commerce, he reported, continued quite brisk, and the flow of goods continued.[105]

The amount or the value of the goods obtained by the Confederacy in and through Mexico cannot be determined. The most important supplies were powder, lead, copper, cloth, beef, flour, and a few small arms and ammunitions from Europe by way of Matamoras. The trade was sufficiently large to act as an effective leverage on obdurate Mexican officials. Neither Vidaurri nor Juarez loved the Confederacy, but the revenue obtained from the commercial relationship prevented any serious overt act. It has been estimated that Vidaurri collected as revenue at Piedras Negras over a million dollars during 1862-1864, and that the revenues on goods at Brownsville and othei depots along

[102] *Ibid.*, April 7, 1864.
[103] *Ibid.*, Quintero to Benjamin, September 5, 1864.
[104] *Ibid.*, October 21, 1864.   [105] *Ibid.*, December 7, 1864.

the border amounted to not less than $125,000 per month.[106] The economic tie was the one that bound.

The trans-Mississippi Department and especially the Texas district profited most from the business. Benjamin, Kirby Smith, President Davis, and the Governors of Texas placed a high estimate on the value of the trade. John Slidell and the Emperor Napoleon were conscious of its importance. The trade across the Rio Grande must have had a significant influence on the life and success of the trans-Mississippi Department.

The real significance of the Mexican developments lies in the possibilities which they offered for prolonging the life of the Confederacy by furnishing a contiguous source of supplies as well as an avenue through which commercial relations with friendly European countries could be maintained. With this situation coming to the front just as the plans for a more efficient handling of purchasing operations in Europe were being worked out and just as new plans in financial arrangements were under discussion, infinite possibilities for the future seemed to present themselves.

The program of centralization and strict governmental regulation of her purchasing operations was not completed until the spring of 1864. The process of making the plan understood, of answering protests, and of demonstrating its effectiveness took several additional months. That the program appealed to European banking interests is attested by the fact that they were willing to negotiate with the Confederacy for a large loan. Preliminary steps in this negotiation, the drafting of contracts, and the clearing of legal impediments were completed late in 1864. But Duncan F. Kenner, to whom the final instructions on the loan were intrusted, did not reach London until the latter part of February, 1865. He was too late. News of military disaster in the South had destroyed all hope of Confederate success. Consequently the full benefit of the New Plan was never

[106] Pickett Papers, Quintero to Benjamin, January 25, 1864; Owsley, *King Cotton Diplomacy*, p. 128.

realized by the South, as it might have been, had the plan been adopted one year earlier. The purchasing agents would have been furnished with abundant credit, the efficiency of the Southern army would have improved, and the military disasters of 1864 and 1865 might have been averted. The military success of the Confederacy had a considerable bearing on her chance of being recognized by European countries. It is impossible to pass final judgment on what might have been the result.

BIBLIOGRAPHY

PRIMARY SOURCES

MANUSCRIPTS

The following are found in the Manuscript Division, Library of Congress:

Correspondence with the Treasury Department. 2 vols.

Mason, James Murray. Correspondence, Documents, etc., 1860-1870.

Volume	I	Jan. 15, 1838—Feb. 8, 1862
"	II	Feb. 10, 1862—July 21, 1862
"	III	July 22, 1862—Dec. 22, 1862
"	IV	Dec. 23, 1862—March 17, 1863
"	V	March 18, 1863—June 16, 1863
"	VI	June 18, 1863—March 7, 1864
"	VII	March 8, 1864—Dec. 16, 1864
"	VIII	Dec. 18, 1864—March 31, 1870

Pickett Papers. Especially the following:

2 vols. of letters from Slidell to Benjamin.

1 vol. of letters from Benjamin to Slidell.

1 vol. containing Hotze's diplomatic correspondence and some private letters.

Package No. 47, containing the "Personal Instructions to the Diplomatic Agents of the Confederate States in Foreign Countries."

Domestic Letters, 2 vols.

Package K, miscellaneous letters from Hotze, De Leon, Helm, and Avegno to the State Department.

Official and personal letters of John T. Pickett, 2 vols.

Volume I May 22, 1849-May 9, 1862

Volume II May 13, 1862-July 5, 1867

"Letter Book," covering miscellaneous correspondence, June 12, 1861-January 13, 1867.

Packages "B" and "C," including Mason's dispatches to the State Department, Nos. 1-46, except nos. 4, 5, 6, 7, and 8. Also miscellaneous private letters of Mason and the dispatches of Mason to the Confederacy from Paris; new series, nos. 1-15.

Letters of J. A. Quintero to Secretary of State, June 1, 1861-Dec. 7, 1864.

Letters of Richard Fitzpatrick to Secretary of State.

Acts and Resolutions of the Confederate States of America. (Manuscript)

Trenholm, George A. Correspondence, etc. 2 portfolios.
Portfolio I   1853-1866
Portfolio II   1867-1897

Willis, Edward (chief quartermaster of General Beauregard's Division).
Letters, Dispatches, Blockade Running, etc. 13 vols. of pamphlets.

GOVERNMENT PUBLICATIONS

Official Records of the Union and Confederate Navies. 31 vols. Government Printing Office, Washington, 1894-1927.

Senate Document, Ser. 987, 62nd Congress, 3rd session. Government Printing Office, Washington, 1913

Senate Report, Ser. 156, 41st Congress, 2nd session. Government Printing Office, Washington, 1870.

War of the Rebellion: Official Records of the Union and Confederate Armies. 130 vols. Government Printing Office, Washington, 1880-1901.

SECONDARY SOURCES

Bigelow, John. *France and the Confederate Navy.* New York. Harper and Brothers, 1888.

———. *Retrospections of an Active Life.* 5 vols. New York. The Baker and Taylor Company, 1909.

Bradbeer, William W. *Confederate and Southern State Currency.* Mt. Vernon, New York, 1915.

Bradlee, Francis B. C. *Blockade Running During the Civil War and the Effect of Land and Water Transportation on the Confederacy.* Salem, Mass. Essex Institute, 1925.

Bulloch, James D. *The Secret Service of the Confederate States in Europe.* 2 vols. London. Richard Bentley and Son, 1883. New York. G. P. Putnam's Sons, 1883.

Capers, Henry D. *The Life and Times of C. G. Memminger.* Richmond. Everett Waddey Company, 1893.

Coulter, E. Merton. "Commercial Intercourse with the Confederacy in the Mississippi Valley, 1861-1865." *Mississippi Valley Historical Review,* V (March, 1919), 377-95.

Green, Duff. *Facts and Suggestions Relative to Finance & Currency*. Augusta, Georgia. J. T. Paterson and Company, 1864.

Hayden, Horace E. *A Refutation of the Charges Made Against the Confederate States of America*. Richmond. G. W. Gary, 1879.

Holladay, Florence E. "The Powers of the Commander of the Confederate Trans-Mississippi Department." *The Southwestern Historical Quarterly*, XXI (January, 1918), 279-98; XXI (April, 1918), 333-59.

Huse, Caleb. *The Supplies for the Confederate Army*. Boston. T. R. Marvin and Son, 1904.

Noll, Arthur. *General Kirby-Smith*. Sewanee, Tennessee. The University Press, 1907.

Latané, John Holladay. *A History of American Foreign Policy*. Garden City, New York. Doubleday, Doran and Co., 1929.

Oldham, W. S. *Speech of Hon. W. S. Oldham, of Texas, on the Subject of the Finances*. Senate, December 23, 1863. Pamphlet.

Owsley, Frank Lawrence. *King Cotton Diplomacy*. Chicago. The University of Chicago Press, 1931.

―――. *State Rights in the Confederacy*. Chicago. The University of Chicago Press, 1925.

Priestley, Herbert I. *The Mexican Nation*. New York. The Macmillan Company, 1923.

Ramsdell, Charles W. "The Texas Military Boards, 1862-1865." *The Southwestern Historical Quarterly*, XXVII, 253-76.

Rippy, J. Fred. *The United States and Mexico*. (Volume XI. Borzoi Historical Series). New York. A. A. Knopf, 1926.

Scharf, John T. *History of the Confederate States Navy from its Organization to the Surrender of its Last Vessel*. San Francisco. A. L. Bancroft & Company, 1887; New York. Rogers and Sherwood, 1887.

Schwab, John C. *The Confederate States of America 1861-1865; A Financial and Industrial History of the South during the Civil War*. New York. C. Scribner's Sons, 1901.

Sellers, James L. "An Interpretation of Civil War Finance." *American Historical Review*, XXX (January, 1925), 282-97.

Smith, Ernest A. "The History of the Confederate Treasury." *Southern History Association*, V (January, 1901), 1-34; V (March, 1901), 99-150; VI (May, 1901), 188-227.

Soley, James Russell. *The Blockade and Cruisers (The Navy in the Civil War*, Vol. I). New York. C. Scribner's Sons, 1885.

Spence, James. *On the Recognition of the Southern Confederation*. Third edition. London. Richard Bentley, 1862.

Watson, William. *The Adventures of a Blockade Runner.* London. T. F. Unwin, 1892.

Wood, Robert C. *Confederate Hand-book.* New Orleans. Graham Press, 1900.

INDEX

State Agents. *See* Agents.

State Rights, 5-6, 48.

"Stephen Hart," sailing vessel, 18, 21, 43.

"Stonewall," cruiser, 40.

Tamaulipas, Mexican state, 104, 108, 121.

Taylor, Major General, 109.

Temporary Plan, 5-6, 7-12, 22, 23. *See also* Financial policy, Cotton, Blockade running and Huse.

Terrell, A. W., and the "Texas Cotton Office," 111.

Texas, 94, 103; trade with Mexico, 108 ff.; cotton office, 111; competes with Confederacy, 114 ff.; border raids, 119 ff. *See also* Mexico, and Trans-Mississippi Department.

Thayer, C. C., and Mexican debt, 123 ff.

Thomson, George, and iron-clads, 33, 34.

Thomson, James, 33, 34.

Times, English newspaper, 62.

Toombs, Robert, and Mexican policies, 105 ff.

Trade Routes, Mexico and Trans-Mississippi Department, 110-11.

Trans-Mississippi Department, 81, 103 ff., 108-10. *See also* Kirby

Smith, Shreveport, Mexico, and Texas.

Trenholm Brothers, 9 ff. *See also* Temporary Plan and Financial policy.

Trenholm, G. A., 9, 90 ff., 96, 100 ff. *See also* Financial policy, Loans, and New Plan.

Vera Cruz, 104-6.

Vidaurri, Santiago, governor of border states, 104 ff., 124 ff.

Voruz, M. J., 39.

Walker, N. S., 8, 43, 51.

Walker, Secretary of War, 17 ff.

"Warrior," iron-clad, 34.

Wilkinson, John, agent for Navy, 31.

Willie, A. H., 115.

Willis, Edward, Quartermaster's department, 44 ff.

Wilmington, 32, 42, 94, 98. *See also* Blockade running, Cotton, and Munitions.

Yancey, William L., Confederate Commissioner, 13.

Zapata, bandit chieftain, 119 ff.

Zuloaga, General, 104 ff.